Canadian Fiction Studies

Additional volumes are in preparation

Orpheus in Winter:
MORLEY CALLAGHAN'S

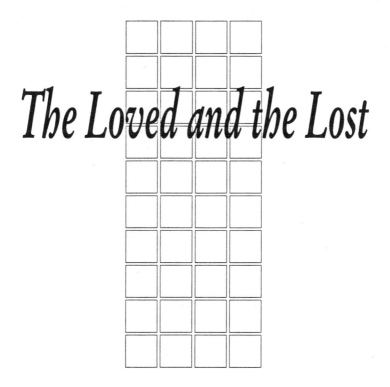

The Loved and the Lost

John Orange

E C W   P R E S S

CHAMPLAIN COLLEGE

Copyright © ECW PRESS, 1993

CANADIAN CATALOGUING IN PUBLICATION DATA

Orange, John
Orpheus in winter : Morley Callaghan's The Loved and the Lost

(Canadian fiction studies ; no. 22)
Includes bibliographic references and index.
ISBN 1-55022-123-X

1. Callaghan, Morley, 1903-1990.
The loved and the lost.
I. Title. II. Series.

PS8505.A43L636 1993   C813'.54   C91-095015-6
PR9199.3.C35L636 1993

This book has been published with the assistance of the
Ministry of Culture, Recreation and Tourism of the Province
of Ontario, through funds provided by the Ontario
Publishing Centre, and with the assistance of grants from
The Canada Council, the Ontario Arts Council, and the
Government of Canada through the Department of
Communications, and the Canadian Studies and Special Projects
Directorate of the Department of the Secretary of State of Canada.

The cover features a reproduction of the dust-wrapper of the
first edition of *The Loved and the Lost*, courtesy of the
Thomas Fisher Rare Book Library, University of Toronto.
Frontispiece photograph courtesy of the Thomas Fisher
Rare Book Library, University of Toronto.
Design and imaging by ECW Type & Art, Oakville, Ontario.
Printed and bound by Kromar Printing, Winnipeg, Manitoba.

Distributed by General Distribution Services,
30 Lesmill Road, Don Mills, Ontario M3B 2T6.

Published by ECW PRESS,
1980 Queen Street East,
Toronto, Ontario M4L 1J2.

□ *Table of Contents* □

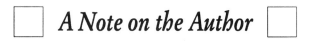

A Note on the Author

John Orange specialized in Canadian Literature and fiction at the University of Toronto where he wrote an M.A. thesis on Callaghan's works and a Phil. M. thesis on the fiction of Ernest Buckler. Since 1970 he has been teaching Canadian Literature at King's College, University of Western Ontario. He has published articles and reviews on those writers as well as on Alice Munro, Hugh Hood, P.K. Page, and others. He has also co-edited the Canadian edition of *The Macmillan Handbook of English*.

A NOTE ON THE TEXT

The Loved and the Lost was first published in Canada by Macmillan in 1951 and it won the Governor-General's Award for fiction for that year. The New American Library (Signet) brought out an edition in the U.S. the next year, and MacGibbon and Kee of London, England issued an edition in 1961. That same year Macmillan reprinted its hard cover edition. Again in England, New English Library published the novel as No. 1624 in its Four Square Books series in 1966, and Macmillan (Canada) issued a paperback edition in its Laurentian Library series (No. 9) in 1970, reprinted in 1983. It has been published in Germany, translated into Russian in 1972 and into Bulgarian in 1977. The most accessible edition, and the one used for this study, is the Macmillan Paperback 37 (1989) which follows the same pagination as the Laurentian Library edition.

In 1955 the novel was adapted as a Broadway musical by Albert Moritz (music) and Thomas Chastain (lyrics) but never performed for financial reasons. It was also adapted for radio by Charles Israel and broadcast on the CBC *Stage* series in three parts in December 1963 and January 1964.

Orpheus in Winter:
Morley Callaghan's
The Loved and the Lost

Chronology

1903   Edward Morley Callaghan born February 22 in Toronto, Ontario to Thomas and Mary (Dewan) Callaghan.

1909–16   Attends Withrow Public School, grades 1–8. Some summers spent in Collingwood — a setting in future novels.

1917–21   Student at Riverdale Collegiate. Summer job selling magazines in the Ottawa Valley.

1921   Publishes first article in Toronto's *Star Weekly*. Enters St. Michael's College at the University of Toronto in Arts. Loves sports and debating.

1923   Works for four summers on the *Toronto Daily Star* as a reporter where he meets Hemingway.

1924   Hemingway shows Callaghan stories to Ford Maddox Ford in Paris and he contacts Callaghan. Meets Loretto Dee at a dance in college.

1925   Graduates from St. Michael's College with BA and enters Osgoode Hall Law School, Toronto. Articles with law firm of Joe Sedgewick.

1926   Publishes first short story in *This Quarter* (Paris); begins to network with literary people in New York.

1927   Begins publishing short stories internationally.

1928   Graduates from Osgoode and is admitted to Ontario Bar. Meets Max Perkins of Scribner's Sons (New York) who publishes short stories and *Strange Fugitive*.

1929   *A Native Argosy*. Marries Loretto Dee whom he had met at College in 1924. Spent summer in Paris where they met various expatriate writers, and boxes with Hemingway in celebrated incident.

1930   *It's Never Over*. Spends most of the year in Pennsylvania and New York writing short stories. Moves finally to Toronto.

1931   *No Man's Meat* published in Paris.

1932   *A Broken Journey*. Son Michael born.

1933   Meets Jacques Maritain, Roman Catholic philosopher.

1934   *Such Is My Beloved.*

1935   *They Shall Inherit the Earth* (banned by Toronto Public Library).

1936   *Now That April's Here and Other Stories*. Lives in New York for six months. (Bank robber Red Ryan shot by police during liquor store hold-up in Sarnia. He had been on parole for less than a year after 11 years in prison.)

1937   *More Joy in Heaven* (based on Red Ryan story). Son Barry born.

1938–47   Engaged in writing articles for *New World* magazine, plays (*Turn Home Again* and *Just Ask for George*) and reviews. A "period of spiritual dryness." Also joined the on-air staff of CBC radio program "Of Things to Come" (renamed "The Citizen's Forum") and in 1947 joined panel of quiz show "Beat the Champs." Sports Editor of *New World Illustrated* from 1940–43; Editorial Associate, 1943–44. Associate Editor of *New World* from 1944 to 1948 and contributes a regular column. Older brother, Burke, dies in 1946 at the age of 44.

1948   Began writing *The Loved and the Lost*. Publishes *Luke Baldwin's Vow* and *The Varsity Story*. Father dies.

1950   Works on radio ("Now I Ask You") and television ("Fighting Words") as regular panellist for the next few years. Mother dies.

1951   *The Loved and the Lost*. Receives Governor General's Award for fiction in the next year.

1952   Moves into house in Rosedale, Toronto.

1955   *The Loved and the Lost* adapted for Broadway as a musical but never performed. "The Man With the Coat" (novella), which wins *Maclean's* $5,000 award. Becomes a regular contributor to CBC *Anthology* series to 1983.

1957	American critic, Edmund Wilson, visits and is impressed with *The Loved and the Lost*.
1958	Three short stories made into a movie that shows at Towne Cinema in Toronto. Visits Rome to cover election of Pope John XXIII for *Toronto Star Weekly*.
1959	*Morley Callaghan's Stories*.
1960	*The Many Colored Coat*. Awarded the Lorne Pierce Medal for Literature by the Royal Society of Canada. Edmund Wilson piece on Callaghan appears in *The New Yorker*.
1961	*A Passion in Rome*. Civic Award of Merit, Toronto.
1963	*That Summer in Paris*.
1964	*More Joy in Heaven* adapted and shown on CBC TV.
1965	Awarded honourary doctorate by University of Western Ontario.
1966	Awarded honourary doctorate by University of Toronto. Canada Council Medal.
1967	Officer of Order of Canada (declined).
1970	Receives the $15,000 Molson Prize and $50,000 Royal Bank Award.
1973	*An Autumn Penitent*. Awarded honourary doctorate by University of Windsor.
1974	*Winter* — non-fiction with photographs.
1975	*A Fine and Private Place*.
1976	First performance of *Season of the Witch* in Peterborough. Revised as a monograph and published.
1977	*Close to the Sun Again*.
1978	*No Man's Meat* and *The Enchanted Pimp*.
1982	Companion of the Order of Canada.
1983	*A Time for Judas*. Media celebrates his 80th birthday.
1984	His wife, Loretto, dies.
1985	*Our Lady of the Snows* and *The Lost and Found Stories of Morley Callaghan*.
1987	CBC makes a film about him, *First Person Singular*.
1987	*The Man with the Coat* published in book form.

1988	*A Wild Old Man on the Road.* A tribute to Callaghan at the first Wang International Festival of Authors.
1989	Toronto Arts Award and Ontario Award for excellence
1990	Dies on August 25.

The Importance of the Work

At a Conference on the Canadian Novel held in Calgary in 1978, a group of teachers and writers compiled by vote a top one-hundred list of significant Canadian novels. Five of Callaghan's novels made the list and *The Loved and the Lost* was close to the first ten titles in the balloting. So far, this novel has been generally considered his best. Exactly why this is so is not that clear. Its form is relatively conventional; its style is somewhat old-fashioned even for 1951. It has never been considered a landmark in Canadian fiction. Yet it continues to be taught in high schools and universities and sells well in paperback.

A novel can be important to its author, its national culture, or to a wider readership. It was an important novel for Callaghan in that it brought him out of the doldrums of 1937–1947 period. As we shall see, the war years had diverted his attention away from the writing of fiction in favour of reviews, articles, and plays. The summers he was spending in Montreal, however, provided a stimulus to writing about a new place, resulting in the new novel, *The Loved and the Lost*. The Governor General's Award the novel received encouraged him to carry on. The novel also indicated a shift in Callaghan's approach to his fiction. The previous novels of the thirties displayed titles taken from the Bible, and these biblical associations were designed to help focus the theme. The structures fit a static formula: an event establishes a moral conflict in the central character; other characters represent options for escape; the protagonist chooses to follow his instinct for love and is forced to make a sacrifice in the process. The hero's choice is the author's choice. Despite some ambiguity in the ending, the didactic purpose of the novel is achieved. With *The Loved and the Lost*, however, the formula all but evaporates and in its place emerges a far more sophisticated and more tightly structured novel. Gone are the biblical guideposts, the ideo-

13

logically stated options, the saintly protagonists. Also the setting is now specific and symbolically functional, whereas in earlier works settings had been vague backdrops. Aesthetically, the novel is Callaghan's most controlled; it "works" the best. Only *Close to the Sun Again* and possibly *Our Lady of the Snows* (some would say *The Many Colored Coat*) succeed as well. In as much as Callaghan is an important writer in the history of Canadian fiction, this novel is both representative of the kind of fiction he is known for and the best example of his artistic skill.

The novel is important, too, for its descriptions of how life is lived in a particular time and place. It is not a historical novel, nor does it try to deal with the whole of Montreal, but it does capture a way of life, a set of attitudes and a way of perceiving events, that was characteristic of Canadian cities when they still had a sense of community — when reputation, class, gossip, made a difference to the people who lived there. The relationships among the characters, their concerns and biases, even their rather wooden dialogue, along with the tone of the narration, taken altogether present an enclosed "world" that captures the parochialism, the class divisions, the ambitions and fears, of a people in the last stages of emerging from their colonial chrysalis. Callaghan has been unjustly ignored as a writer of cultural history because he does not add a great deal of detail to his descriptions. However, he is interested more in capturing intangibles such as mood, atmosphere, the tone of an era; in these respects, this novel is a successful recreation of the times.

It should be kept in mind, too, that the treatment of racial prejudice is fairly rare in our fiction, though racism and prejudice can be found in many places in our history and culture. *The Loved and the Lost* is, among other things, an examination of the racial and ethnic conflicts that simmer beneath the surface in our big cities — conflicts we have traditionally denied. Callaghan faced the issue in this novel at a time when accusations of racism based on class and economic deprivation were dismissed as unfounded by most Canadians.

Finally, the importance of the novel rests on its more universal appeal. It has been successful in the U.S. and in England and so far it has been translated into German, Russian, and Bulgarian. There are a number of elements in the novel that touch readers no matter where they are. Callaghan always stressed the dignity of the individual over social imperatives. He insisted that the wonder, the eagerness, the inner glow (to use words he was fond of) that makes life worthwhile need not be extinguished by life's disappointments as we grow older. Callaghan believed in the possibility of defending one's inner light against those who want us to compromise; his writing investigated how we succeed and fail in this crucial enterprise. These are themes that transcend time and place. At the same time, his novels usually involve sensational events — murder, prostitution, assault, suicide, slander, betrayal, homosexuality, and the melodrama that accompanies them. He has always had a strong cigar store bookstand appeal. His style, however, is relatively bland and quiet in direct contrast to his content. This creates odd combinations: involvement and detachment, journalistic realism and artifice, didacticism and irony, moral persuasion and ambiguity. Eventually the experience of the text begins to feel like life itself, no matter how frustrating or inappropriate it may feel as artistry.

This final "feel" of the text is completely in keeping with Callaghan's own philosophy which remained adamantly anti-intellectual, anti-ideological, anti-Establishment. The human spirit resists static paradigms in Callaghan's view; his mission was to find a form and style to convey this wider notion in the narrower context of ordinary events. His meditations on moral courage in individual lives ultimately point us in the direction of the possibility of the transcendence of the human spirit. These are notions that Callaghan expresses in *The Loved and the Lost* in refined ways. In *That Summer in Paris* Callaghan described how he attempted to develop a prose that would illuminate his vision:

I remember one time at twilight, sitting at the typewriter in the sunroom of my parents' home. I could smell the lilacs. A night bird cried. A woman's voice came from a neighbour's yard. I wanted to get it down so directly that it wouldn't feel or look like literature. I remembered too being with a girl one night, and on the way home, walking alone, I felt the world had been brought close to me; there seemed to be magic in the sound of my own footsteps, even in the noise of the streetcars — all mingled with the girl's kiss, the memory of the little run I had noticed in her stocking, the way she had said good-bye to me. None of it had to be written up. There it was, beautiful in itself. A "literary guy" would spoil it. (18)

Later on he writes about his impatience with traditional religious dualism:

> My own problem was to relate a Christian enlightenment to some timeless process of becoming. A disgust with the flesh born of an alleged awareness of an approaching doomsday bored me, as did the flash of light that gave a man the arrogant assurance that he was the elect of God. (89–90)

His purpose in writing, in light of all of this, was to

> strip the language, and make the style, the method, all the psychological ramifications, the ambience of the relationships, all the one thing, so the reader couldn't make separations. Cézanne's apples. The appleness of apples. Yet just apples. (145)

Whether or not he achieves what he says he set out to do in his writing has been debated vigorously and continually. The disagreement about Callaghan's success as a writer will probably never be solved. His ambitions themselves are important enough for him to be taken seriously, and his influence on the development of fiction in Canada is well established. Since *The Loved and the Lost* represents his writing at its best, since the novel carries with it his earlier and later traits, since it is carefully crafted and has obvious wide appeal, it is safe to say that it is an important novel in itself and for its place in Callaghan's canon as well as in Canadian letters in general.

Critical Reception

Initially, *The Loved and the Lost* was not received well at all. It was turned down by eight different publishers before it was accepted by Macmillan in New York and Toronto. The hard-cover edition sold only a few thousand copies. Callaghan himself was baffled by its reception. Except for encouraging letters from Maritain, Hans Selye, and other writers, he felt misunderstood. A few reviews were favourable, but many were lukewarm or even hostile. In 1952, however, the Signet New American Library fifty-cent paperback edition of 300,000 copies sold out after eight years and a second edition of 175,000 copies was printed. It took time to catch on, but it has since sustained a popularity that has grown slowly and steadily. The criticism of the novel has followed the same pattern.

The kind of evaluation and interpretation that a work receives will often depend upon the kind of questions the reader chooses to ask. William Arthur Deacon, reviewing for *The Globe and Mail*, for example, asked whether or not the novel was a true tragedy. He concluded that the people involved in the story, especially Peggy Sanderson, were too confused to have heroic qualities, nor were any great passions or principles at stake. He admired its craftsmanship but objected to Peggy as "not worth the uproar" (10). Victor Hass of the *Chicago Tribune* agreed, calling Jim McAlpine "a fatuous numskull" and Peggy "an odd stick and a tramp in the bargain" (6). Bernard Sandwell felt that it was not a great novel because the characters were so ordinary that Peggy's death was not really tragic. *The New York Times Review* found the story "romantic, implausible" (18), while the *revue de l'Université Laval* wanted to know more about Peggy in order to explain her life and death (52). Other reviewers asked a slightly different set of questions, usually a variant on: how realistic were the novel's elements? Mary Ross, in the *New*

York Herald Tribune Books found Callaghan's restraint in dealing with an explosive issue admirable and Peggy an unforgettable character (6). Claude Bissell in his annual review of Canadian writing was one of the few voices to praise the novel not only as Callaghan's best to date but also "one of the best contemporary Canadian novels" (260). Most of the praise for the novel was reserved for its direct style and firm structure — qualities which, over time, have actually come to be perceived as weaknesses of the work by some critics. The conflict between content and style, implicit didactic purpose (parable form) and final outcome (ambiguity of character and theme), begins, in its small way, by the two kinds of questions asked in these reviews.

Most of the subsequent examinations of the novel were tucked into more general studies of Callaghan's works. In a 1957 article, Hugo McPherson admired the way the symbols, chosen from the setting, created two worlds, Peggy's and Jim's. These symbols structure the action. For McPherson, Peggy represents "the intuitive knowledge Love is the way to blessedness," while Jim represents the "temporal order." "The whole action of the drama concerns the possibility of the two orbits merging — a possibility which is almost fulfilled" (Conron 1975, 71). Jim tries to be part of her serenity but cannot maintain his faith in what she believes in and tragically, she is destroyed "by the forces of this world" — human nature and various social orders acting together. Jim's search for the church at the end of the novel is a search for "the source of Peggy's secret radiance" (Conron 1975, 73). This essentially religious reading of the novel establishes a romantic view of Peggy as a Saint Joan martyred by secular forces. McPherson's analysis established the way the novel would be read by most of the later critics.

A few years later in a summary article on Callaghan, George Woodcock outlined what he felt were the novel's weaknesses — an unsuccessful combining of the conventions of the social novel (its realism and topic of racism) and romance (its quest motif for the holy grail and Orpheus myth), an indistinctly embodied moral theme, and a description of two worlds neither of which is "convincing or consistent" (Conron 1975, 100). In the same year (1964), Edmund Wilson, in his book *O Canada*, came to the opposite conclusion. He described Peggy as saintly, and praised Callaghan for never sacrificing her believability by lapsing into mysticism or sentimentality. Wilson was confident that Peggy is virginal, independent and idealistic and is killed by Walter Malone. She represents "reckless devotion to a Christian ideal of love which is bound to come to grief in the world" (Conron 1975, 119). His view of Callaghan is that he is a "deeply if undogmatically Christian" writer. Even early on, critics see-sawed between interpreting Peggy as representing a Christian ideal doomed to Christ-like destruction, or as an enigma at best who only confuses issues.

In his 1966 book on Callaghan, Brandon Conron agreed with McPherson's notion of two worlds, and he developed an analysis of the novel's structure based on a dialectic of contrasts. On the one side there is Peggy, her intuitive perception of life based on "the spiritual values by which man should live" (Conron 1966, 128), her self-renouncing childhood experience, the river, the church, white and blonde colours, the St. Antoine Café, the factory workers. On the other side of the dialectic are Jim, the mountain and cross of security and intellectual order, social conventions, his self-willed childhood experience, the leopard, darkness and black colours, the Earbenders Club and the Carvers. Jim represents the Christian man, alienated and alone in the modern world, torn between the conflicting values represented in the dialectic — essentially Peggy versus Catherine. For Conron, the novel finally asserts the triumph of love. Peggy is a complex character, purposefully left ambiguous, but ultimately she dies resisting evil and her spirit returns to comfort Jim as he searches for the little church, "a symbol of genuine Christian love" (Conron 1966, 130). [Callaghan shows "psychological perceptiveness and "his restraint and sure sense of dialogue bring all the various characters to life," as well, the central characters are "especially vital" (Conron 1966, 133–34).] Conron found the treatment of Catherine to be particularly subtle and sympathetic while Peggy is made plausible by her untidiness, failure of judgement, warmth, and provocative behaviour. His admiration of structure and characterization are the very things later critics found objectionable.

In 1968, John Matthews saw in Peggy, "an emblem of moral synthesis, refusing classification, she attempts to hold intact the fusion between inner and outer reality — the outward sign and the inner grace (the leopard and church symbols)" (44), but she cannot survive in a society that insists on judging only by appearances. Since Canadian society has not found a way to integrate private visions into an overriding mythology, we require an act of faith in the individual. Peggy dies because of Jim's failure of faith in her and the whole novel inadvertently becomes an allegory on the Canadian colonial condition (47). Matthews was the first to try to tie the novel into a specifically Canadian cultural context.

Victor Hoar (1969) again defines two worlds in the novel and sees McAlpine as suspended in the limbo between them called the Chalet Restaurant. He sees Jim as attempting to impose his order on Peggy's life. Her resistance and final destruction moves him from self-interest and egotism to mercy and compassion. Peggy has found a way to reconcile Manichean dichotomies of Light versus Darkness, soul versus body, carnal life versus spiritual life, but Jim can't realize that to save her on his terms is to destroy her on hers. Hoar finds Jim to be irritating, naïve, and stupid, a man who preaches existentialism and is no existentialist himself. He finds Peggy complex ("Eve one second after the fall"), her innocence too much for the world, her indiscrimination "an enormous capacity for love" (116). However, there are too many obviously imposed images and symbols such as the white horse. Altogether they interrupt the flow of the narrative. It also seems implausible that McAlpine would make any impression on Peggy in the first place.

Doug Jones, in his overview of patterns in Canadian literature, *Butterfly on Rock*, sees Peggy as an archetypal female figure associated with the rejection of the garrison culture — a figure prevalent in Canadian writing. He defines her approach to life as inclusive of opposites and without fear, as opposed to McAlpine and Company who believe that social order depends on barriers of class or race. McAlpine cannot share her understanding of how church and leopard go together, so his failure of faith means his loss of joy in life. A return to spring and conventional social order makes him Adam separated from Eve — "the passion and the mystery which gave to life its intensity and its depth." This description of Peggy raises her status a notch to archetypal Life Force, a status that some later critics will follow (54). Jones describes McAlpine's loss as a reflection of the failure of imagination typical of Canada in its colonial phase. He seeks to find a cultural application of the story, the way Matthews did, by focusing on only one aspect of the novel.

In his sweeping article on Callaghan, British critic William Walsh found Callaghan's use of Montreal effective, and he judged McAlpine to be sensitive, honest, open-minded, intelligent and warm-hearted, albeit ambitious. If one compares Victor Hoar's reaction to the same things, one wonders if they were reading the same novel. Since we live inside of Jim's perceptions for most of the story, he represents normality to Walsh. Peggy is true to her own nature (147), so she becomes the standard by which we are to judge those others who live indirectly or deviously, constantly responding to forces outside of themselves. Peggy, on the other hand, is saintly in Walsh's view because her motives are never wholly socially nor genetically conditioned. She relies on spontaneous feeling, and although there is in the account of her "motives a shaded ambiguity which, while it may be lacking in abstract logic, is, one feels, closely in correspondence with the complications of reality" (Conron 1975, 148). Thus the critic brushes aside the problems of her ambiguity as simply put in the service of realism. In fact, Walsh found the combination of difficult moral theme and casually conversational style a "technical achievement." Two years later, Fraser Sutherland dismissed the whole novel as being "simply not credible" (76) because neither Jim nor Peggy make any sense at all, the dialogue is dull, Montreal is unrecognizable, the psychology and sociology weak, and the symbolism is handled heavy-handedly. So went the battle of contradictions about the work.

John Moss's various descriptions of the novel have always been, on balance, on the negative side of the debate. In *Patterns of Isolation*, he senses that Peggy does not really know who she is and it is Jim who is ruined because he is ensnared in a relationship with her. The characters are uninteresting because, for the most part, we never see evidence for what we are told they are. Peggy is coy, determined to maintain her own integrity and Jim is a cliche, but their relationship is dramatically powerful. Moss emphasizes the psychological elements in the novel. Peggy's childhood experience has established "her neurotic predilection for Negroes" which is "an expiating milieu, allowing her an exotic context for her determined pursuit to be her own self" (220). In Moss's view, Jim becomes a "victim of Peggy's own obsessive behaviour" (221) when he commits himself to prove the existence of her innocence — a commitment that is in itself partially rooted in "as Presbyterian a disposition as McAlpine's" (222). The irony in the novel rests on the notion that the world is sustained by guilt. Irony and ambiguity are the only answers provided for the moral tangle. In *A Reader's Guide to Canadian Fiction*, Moss is very critical of Callaghan's style in this novel.

A detailed treatment of Callaghan's social criticism as it appears in the novel can be found in Judith Kendle's penetrating 1976 article entitled "Spiritual Tiredness and Dryness of the Imagination: Social Criticism in the Novels of Morley Callaghan." Callaghan pictures Canadian society as sober, sedate, puritan, hard-working, and materialistic so that the plight of the individual is lost in favour of social authority resulting in collective intolerance of individual differences and "success of the heart" (116). Moral development is stunted as is the development of the imagination and intuition. In the novel, various classes, social groups and generations are represented by various characters. All favour unwarranted respect for conventional order to the extent that gaiety, compassion, warmth, spontaneity, integrity and love cannot grow in this environment. Peggy's individualism transcends economic and social conditioning and Callaghan is on her side in her rejection of social conformity, rationalist faith, religious hypocrisy. By placing absolute trust in her "whirling-away feeling," she is the novel's only individual. However, the real target of the novel is Jim. Questions of how seriously are we to take Peggy's lifestyle, or if she is innocent are largely irrelevant. The key to Jim's failure lies in his clumsy sketches. Callaghan likes to relate artistic sensibility and imagination to conscience. Jim's pencil drawing of Peggy betrays his arrogance and lack of appreciation of her uniqueness just as the Carvers buy paintings for investment purposes.

In another introductory book on Callaghan, Patricia Morley emphasizes the duality in Peggy. "Callaghan's memorable heroine is a generous spirit with a tragic flaw" (Morley 1978, 42). It is a duality which permeates all of the characters, events, and even the structure of the novel. Everything that seems innocent turns guilty when seen from another perspective. The magical white horses turn destructive in Jim's dream just as Peggy courts destruction by her wilful imprudence. The image of the Johnson family is transposed into that of the Negroes who spit and jeer at her; Peggy the innocent idealist brings out the worst in people.

By far the most intricately argued treatment of the novel is contained in David Dooley's book *Moral Vision in the Canadian Novel.* He concentrates on the relationship between the two protagonists to see what can be made of it. If Peggy represents some spiritual value, then Jim's retreat may mean he is missing something important. However, it is not certain that Peggy represents holiness as McPherson, Morley and others would have it. Her presentation from the beginning is ambiguous. She is not the opposite of the leopard, nor does the church represent a religious basis for her love of her fellow-man. It is not clear that she believes in anything except her "whirl-ing-away feelings" which are suspicious theologically and could be an illusion. Her choice of order over disorder is wilful and immature. Jim's love for her makes her concede that there are different kinds of love and that she is going to have to discriminate among them — something she refuses to do. Jim's warnings to her are certainly sensible, just as his misgivings about her are rooted in his insecurity over whether he is loved for himself alone (72). His alleged betrayal of her is simply "a refusal to act as though he were convinced of her love when he is not, a refusal to treat love as a matter for one night rather than for enduring years" (73). Jim's self-incrimination and Callaghan's agreement with it is difficult for readers to accept because it seems unfair since her behaviour is often so questionable. She views religion as something to react *against* and the church is valued for its balance and light rather than for its supernatural aspirations. Cal-laghan never rules out alternative interpretations of Peggy's motives or of what she represents. Nor are we sure whether or not Jim has made a mistake. Has he put too much faith in her or too little? Is he treating an ordinary person as if she were a saint? Is his desertion of her out of moral principle? Dooley concludes by listing the paradoxes in the novel. "Where else can one read," he asks, "about a rejected woman [Catherine] slapping the face of her former lover because he has *not* slept with her rival, and the man in question thinking that he has betrayed a good and holy woman [Peggy] by respecting her chastity?" (77).

In 1980, a symposium was held at the University of Ottawa on Callaghan's writing. There were various approaches taken to his art and some of the debates centred on *The Loved and the Lost*. Ray Ellenwood, for example, felt that McAlpine confuses the social order with the moral order until he meets Peggy, who represents a point of synthesis between good and evil. However, this point of synthesis has to be "a point of great moral ambiguity" (Staines 43), and since Callaghan's main characters are naïve, his books are "relentlessly ironic" (44). The dangerous characters are those who think they can recognize good and evil absolutely. Perhaps even Peggy suffers a little from this. Barry Cameron, at the same meeting, agreed that

Callaghan wrote "moral fiction" and he examined the didactic strategies he uses to make his moral point. Since he uses the conventions of parable, his emphasis is on behaviour, events and relationships as illustrations of an ethical situation, rather than strictly on realistic description or deep character analysis. Parables test the reader and often leave the point of the story for the reader to discover, although Callaghan likes to include remarks like that of Detective Bouchard at the end of the story just to nail it down. In *The Loved and the Lost*, Callaghan is deliberately ambiguous so that we are not sure how to evaluate any of the characters; he accomplishes this by switching his narrative point of view from himself to a variety of characters. We are forced to identify with Jim and his rational approach to Peggy until the betrayal scene when we are directed to separate ourselves from him and to judge him as unfair and redirect our sympathy to Peggy. At this point we see Jim suffering for his lack of intuition, but we have been made to doubt Peggy too because we have followed Jim through the story. The real issue all along is not whether or not Peggy is innocent, but whether Jim believes she is innocent. We discover at the end that we were supposed to be resisting Jim's arguments against Peggy and favouring her intuitive approach all along. However, this was impossible since we were following Jim so closely. Cameron objects to the trick because it is a trick of propaganda deliberately to limit the reader's alternatives by controlling information. In fact, this trick may dislocate the moral effect of the whole novel.

Larry McDonald's position was that Callaghan is *not* a particularly Christian writer at all since there is no reference to an afterlife and the notion of original sin is denied. Callaghan is more influenced by the theories of Freud, Marx and Darwin than he is by Maritain, and although his "Catholicism is present as a structure of feeling" (78), he analyzes man and society in terms of psychology, economics and biology. Whatever is spiritual, religious or transcendent "is always experienced as the full realization of human potential, and is always consistent with a secular moral vision [based in] scientific skepticism .... There is a strong allegorical impulse in his fiction, but its subject is human consciousness, not Christian redemption" (Staines 78). McAlpine, for example, was scarred in his childhood by the rich and powerful; his early experience cannot be escaped. He puts his faith in reason, a product of ego and part of his personal neurosis. Peggy represents the irrational, anarchistic, instinct for life that lies in the unconscious (91) and, like Callaghan, she rejects the dualist or Manichean strain in Christian theology in favour of a monist view of human nature. She is selfless, "unpolluted by anything so tainted as an idea" (Staines 88), committed to wrestle with society's institutionalized values and doomed to fail. McDonald essentially romanticizes Peggy just as Jones, Conron, Matthews, Walsh and others did, but he prefers to evaluate her meaning in a secular rather than a religious context.

Donald Bartlett, in a 1981 essay on Callaghan's treatment of his heroines, asserts that these women are complex and mysterious and that it is precisely these qualities which perplex the heroes and raise the novels above psychology and sociology to tragic literature. We have come full circle from the first reviewer who complained that the novel was not tragic, merely pathetic. Peggy, according to Bartlett's reading, is good, pure, Christ-like in that she is betrayed, misunderstood and destroyed. The leopard suggests her distrust of something in her own nature, as well as Callaghan's awareness of the polarities that make up the human condition. However, the little church indicates that Peggy sees Christianity as the antidote to this savage element in herself and in society and she passes this feeling to Jim. Her judgement of people is poor (she confuses the Johnson family with the negroes of St. Antoine), but she is not perverse. Jim betrayed her to his social ambition but comes away with new self-knowledge.

The most recent treatment of the novel can be found in a book on racism in Canadian fiction by Terrence Craig. He sees Peggy as above race and class, "the first true anti-racist figure in Canadian literature" (106), neither neurotic nor irresponsible, an idealist and an ideal, "not herself too good to be true, but just too good for her society to allow to be true" (104). In fact, Peggy sums up Callaghan's explanation for racism: ethnocentric pride employed individually to supply security and self-confidence for the Carvers, Wolgasts and Wagstaffs of the world. The novel is more about class than race. Jim wants to reclaim her for white society by redecorating her mind and her apartment with European symbols.

All of these interpretations overlap in a variety of areas. Each has something to offer, yet glaring contradictions can be found among them. In all cases, the conclusions depend upon the kinds of questions asked. However, the tendency is to praise or blame Callaghan for the answers to those questions. Most of the critics focus on just what Peggy Sanderson represents or how real she is. The answers to those questions colour the answers to the rest. That the novel can produce so much debate, such impassioned responses, such a variety of approaches, testifies to its richness. Callaghan insisted that a genuine work of art should not be reducible to a formula or a phrase summarizing its theme. It should faithfully reproduce our experience of life itself — its wonder, mystery, frustration and tragedy. On his own terms, at least, he seems to have succeeded.

Reading of the Text

THE AUTHOR'S PERSPECTIVE

In order to appreciate Callaghan's novel fully, one should pay some attention to the way he developed as a writer. Not "liking" a writer's prose, or what he has to say, is one thing, but we should make an effort to "appreciate" these things in the context of what the author set out to do. Callaghan's particular perspective on the world evolved through the late 1920s and 1930s out of a particular reaction to the kind of writing that was popular in the previous era. He seems to have established a kind of prose to suit his purposes by borrowing bits and pieces from here and there and putting them together with his own tastes finally to develop a style that he modified only a little until he wrote *The Loved and the Lost*. A short excursion through his life in order to glance at the forces which shaped him as a writer will help to establish how, at least, Callaghan expects us to read his novel. This is not the last word, of course, since ultimately the novel will have to speak for itself, but some knowledge of the author's ambitions will afford keys into the appreciation of the work.

My first awareness of Morley Callaghan was through his appearances on the CBC television program "Fighting Words" in the late 1950s. He continually disarmed my expectations by rarely ever saying what I anticipated a fellow who looked and acted the way he did would be likely to say. He was a bundle of contradictions: a small, feisty man, overloaded with self-confidence; a man with opinions about virtually everything but never without an ironic glint in his eye; a lawyer who never practised the law: a Roman Catholic who criticized the Church; a man who spoke very simply and plainly about complex concepts; someone who seemed to know famous people but who chose to stay home in Canada living in a kind of exile.

In those days, he was a puzzle to me. When I began to read his stories and novels a decade later, the puzzle deepened not only because the quiet tone and gentle approach in the stories did not fit the personality I had seen, but because the stories themselves did not seem to answer the questions they so insistently posed. As he aged, he became more charming, just as talkative and engaging, something of a legend. His works still attract a wide diversity of critical evaluation. Callaghan himself enjoyed being an enigma, probably because he always felt that important things in life cannot, and should not, be fully understandable.

There is no full biography of Callaghan yet, but he has written about himself directly in *That Summer in Paris*, and indirectly in two novels — *The Varsity Story* and *A Fine and Private Place*. In his numerous essays and interviews he often foregrounded his ideas by recounting anecdotes from his own experiences, so we already know a good deal about his life and his beliefs. Second son of Thomas Callaghan (a Welshman of Irish descent and dispatcher with the CNR), Morley Callaghan was born on February 22, 1903. His mother was from Collingwood, Ontario, and together his parents encouraged their two sons to take an interest in literature, music, and politics. It may be an omen that they named their first son after the famous centrist politician, Edmund Burke, and their second son after Burke's biographer, John Morley, a liberal. A lively clash of ideas was a way of life for Callaghan even when he was young; it is no wonder that he developed into a youth interested in everything that came his way from baseball to poetry. By the time he finished high school he had published an essay in the *Star Weekly* and had begun to take an interest in fiction, although his parents were encouraging him to follow their passion by becoming a politician after going through law school. He read widely, but his preference was for American writers because they were writing about his immediate interests and experiences at the time — sports, neighbours, local gangsters, reporters and politicians.

In the summer of 1923, mid-way through his B.A. at St. Michael's College in the University of Toronto, he quit a job in a lumberyard because he was worried about his pitching arm, and got a job as a reporter on *The Toronto Star* by offering to work a trial week for free. There he first met Ernest Hemingway, who was the paper's European corespondent briefly visiting the Toronto newsroom, and the two men struck up a friendship which included exchanging the stories they had written. The American writer had been developing a lean, spare, journalistic style that must have impressed Callaghan because there are plenty of signs of this style, derived from the newspaper reporting of the day, in Callaghan's early work. Hemingway was impressed enough by Callaghan's stories to carry a number of them back to Paris where he eventually showed them to Bob McAlmon of Contact Editions, Hemingway's first publisher. McAlmon liked Callaghan's work and handed his stories around to other small presses which eventually agreed to publish some of them in 1926. In the meantime, Callaghan graduated, continued to work full-time during the summers, and part-time in the winters, for the newspaper. He went on to Osgoode Hall Law School mostly out of a sense of duty to his parents, because by this time he had decided to become a professional writer.

The Hemingway connection had opened up a network of literary acquaintances including F. Scott Fitzgerald, Ezra Pound, Katherine Anne Porter, Ford Maddox Ford, William Carlos Williams, among the notables. His work was brought to the attention of the influential Max Perkins of Scribner's who asked to see more and eventually agreed to publish some short stories and *Strange Fugitive* in 1928. By the time he was only twenty-six years old, Callaghan was a lawyer, married to Loretto Dee whom he had met at a College dance, a short-story writer already published in Paris and New York, and a novelist whom Scribner's had decided to promote as a rival to Hemingway.

Callaghan's affinity to Hemingway, originally established simply as part of Scribner's marketing strategy, became a short-term asset and a long-term liability. The asset was that Callaghan was accepted into an important literary circle and thus quickly accepted as a serious writer. He obviously needed support outside of Toronto in those days in order to be a professional writer. It also helped to bolster his confidence in his own talents even though he realized early on that any resemblance to Hemingway's "hard-boiled realism" was superficial. The liability was that his work was often misunderstood or damned unjustly for not being enough like Hemingway's. However, in the 1920s, a young man on the rise from Toronto, Ontario would have been foolish to retreat from such an exciting league of players on the grounds that he was being marketed incorrectly. He had learned in College that if one writes the way one talks, writing flows easily. His journalism had trained him to be direct and simple; his lawyer's training had made him focus on factual evidence; his Roman Catholic background had made him attentive to symbols. Add to all of this his reading of contemporary Naturalists, with their blurry Marxist and vaguely Freudian determinism, the emphasis placed on conscience and free will in his religious training, plus the 1920s fashionable anxiety for the underdog, and Callaghan's early influences and style begin to take a rough shape.

A seven-month honeymoon in Paris in 1929, recounted later in his memoir *That Summer in Paris*, seemed to force Callaghan to define more clearly for himself just how he fit in as a writer with the ex-patriot generation of the twenties. (A little boxing match with Hemingway, mistimed by Fitzgerald, resulted in Hemingway on the mat, and it seems he never forgave Callaghan. Callaghan wrote about the event later but complained that that little bout seemed to trap his reputation in the past when he felt his writing and his present were far more important.) He completed a novella, *No Man's Meat*, and started a novel, *It's Never Over*, before returning to North America with a strong sense of his differences from his contemporaries. He and his wife commuted for eight months between a farm house in Pennsylvania and a hotel in New York City while he wrote short stories, before they settled in Toronto. His decision to live in Toronto was a measure of Callaghan's balanced judgement. He grew up in the Riverdale district; he knew these people, and he could work there well enough. He knew what he was about. He roamed around Toronto talking to people "from the other side of the tracks" — people who moved and interested him as much as they would from anywhere else. Although the group interested in literature in the thirties was small, still everyone knew each other in the lobby of the Royal, and parties with Mazo de la Roche at Lady Willison's, conversations with Pelham Edgar, or dress-up affairs at Hugh Eayrs, president of Macmillans, made up a cozy group of encouraging friends. Besides, most magazines still published short stories, and New York was never all that far away.

During the Depression, in this relatively quiet setting, Callaghan was very productive. He published five novels and a novella, a collection of stories, and dozens of reviews, as well as writing two plays. Both of his sons were born in this decade, and his reputation as a controversial author who wrote about moral and spiritual courage grew internationally. His fictional characters gradually became more complex as their social and psychological situations became increasingly conflicted. External authority represented by the law, Church, role responsibilities, are presented in the novels as undermining subjective perceptions of personal fulfilment, and the resulting moral dilemmas are presented as case studies in spiritual growth or failure. The stories can be read as parables in which the behaviour of the characters invites the reader to meditate on the moral truths hidden inside the story. References to the Bible underscore the stories' structures and themes, though they rarely ever define the answers to the questions raised. From *It's Never Over* through *A Broken Journey, Such Is My Beloved, They Shall Inherit the Earth*, and *More Joy in Heaven* (based on the story of the bank robber, Red Ryan, who was gunned down by police during a liquor store holdup), Callaghan continued to investigate and refine his themes: the sanctity of individual integrity inevitably frustrated by the pressures of social organization; the presence of the remarkable in ordinary lives; the ambiguities hidden in what are generally considered to be simple virtues — innocence, justice, prudence, loyalty, progress, ambition, passionate idealism, even love. Callaghan had become friends with the French philosopher Jacques Maritain who was lecturing at St. Michael's College in 1933–34 — an association that continued for many years and one that provides clues, but not final answers, to Callaghan's vision of human destiny. One other event of note in the thirties is Callaghan's departure from Scribner's in 1934 in favour of Random House. He had never sold well at Scribner's, and Bennett Cerf offered him more money and better distribution.

Partly because of the rise of Fascism in Spain, Italy, and Germany, and Communism in Russia, partly because of the depressing events of the ensuing World War, from 1938 to 1948 Callaghan found it too difficult to write stories describing the subtleties of the moral dilemmas of ordinary people in such extraordinary times. He kept busy by working on articles, reviews, plays, and radio. He adapted *They Shall Inherit the Earth* into a play called "Going Home" for the New York Theatre Guild (eventually performed in Toronto in 1950), and penned a new play entitled "To Tell the Truth" which was also billed to be performed in New York but was put aside until it was performed in Toronto in the spring of 1949. He knew many people on

31

Broadway and was offered a job as a Hollywood screenwriter which he turned down for a variety of reasons. In a nutshell, he took up his journalism career again by becoming a feature writer and sports columnist for a number of magazines and the chairman of a CBC radio program best known as "Citizen's Forum" which took him back and forth across Canada debating issues of local concern. In 1947 he was invited to join the panel of the radio show called "Beat the Champs," and his engaging personality and debating skills led him to regular work on a radio show called "Now I Ask You," and in the fifties to "Anthology" on radio and "Fighting Words" on television. He was restless to find a new milieu after the war. He had spent some summers in Montreal at the end of the forties with his friend, sports editor Dink Carroll, when their wives were at a cottage. The experience of that city, plus the realization that he was going nowhere as a playwright, jolted him awake. He took up writing fiction again.

The acceptance of his story originally entitled "The Little Business Man" by *The Saturday Evening Post* in 1947, and the publisher's suggestion that it be expanded into a novel, along with an invitation to write something for the University of Toronto's fund raising campaign in 1948, resulted in the publication of *Luke Baldwin's Vow* and *The Varsity Story* — signals of Callaghan's renewed commitment to his original goal to be a great writer. He began working on *The Loved and the Lost*, set in Montreal, late in the same year and finished it two years later. It won the Governor General's Award for fiction for 1951. His experience of Montreal, in fact, stimulated another story, "The Man with the Coat" (1955), which also won a prize and was rewritten as *The Many Colored Coat* published in 1959. However, after 1953 there were virtually no more short stories because Callaghan had decided he had done all he could do with the form. Many of his critics still feel that his short stories are his best writing since the form and his subjects seem to go so well together.

A trip to Rome in 1958 to cover the election of a new pope gave him ideas for his next novel, *A Passion in Rome*. The central characters in these novels were more hardened and more sophisticated than his earlier ones; the irony and ambiguity are closer to the surface. Most readers found the endings perplexing. The novels received very mixed reviews, infuriating some reviewers and bewildering others. In 1960 a profile of Callaghan by the influential critic Edmund Wilson appeared in the *New Yorker*. Wilson claimed that Callaghan may be the most underestimated writer of the century. That year he also received the Lorne Pierce Medal for Literature from the Royal Society of Canada. His reputation was secure, but his novels continued to elicit everything from praise to indifference to vituperation. The suicide of Hemingway in 1961 revitalized interest in the relationship between the men and stimulated Callaghan to return to his work on his Paris memoirs. *That Summer in Paris* provoked the usual mixed reaction, but it did afford its author an opportunity to explain what goes into his writing. He seemed anxious to be better understood and to rid himself of the too close affinity with Hemingway which dogged his career.

With the exception of a handful of essays and reviews, Callaghan wrote very little between 1963 and 1974. He worked mostly on radio and television, reading his works and resting on his reputation. He turned down the Canadian Government's offer to make him an "Officer" of the Order of Canada because he saw the award as second class since it was a step below the "Companion" level — a further indication of the self-confidence he sustained from the beginning of his career. It was not until 1982 that he was given the Companion of the Order of Canada award. In the meantime he received honorary doctorates from universities and large cash prizes from corporations for his contribution to the arts in Canada. The accolades impressed upon him that he was becoming something of a pressed flower, so he went back to writing novels. *A Fine and Private Place* (1975) was his version of the post-modern trend to write about writing itself. Callaghan concocted an elaborate self-reflexive novel about a novelist very much like himself under scrutiny by a graduate student who is studying his work. It can even be read as a send-up of postmodernist literary assertions. Part hoax, part serious meditation on aging, the novel stirred up the critics again. Since then he has published seven new books, *Close to the Sun Again, A Time for Judas*, based on the Biblical character, *Our Lady of the Snows*, and *A Wild Old Man on the Road*, as well as revised versions of earlier novels, and a collection of early unpublished stories. The man who was successful before he was twenty-five was his most prolific after the age of seventy and into his late eighties!

The confidence Callaghan had in himself, the commitment he made to writing, the stubbornness with which he sustained his talent, impressed upon Canadians of his generation (not without some resentment along the way) that perhaps we were worth writing about, that we could produce a writer of international stature. His success inspired the next generation of writers to forge ahead unapologetically. It is fair to say that Callaghan left a legacy that is far larger than his impressive list of titles. For over sixty years he maintained his initial assertions that one has to be loyal to one's perceptions, faithful to one's own lights. Our national culture is the livelier for his example. He died on Saturday, August 25, 1990, at the age of eighty-seven. He will be known as the writer who brought the world to Canadian fiction and Canadian fiction to the world.

THE QUESTION OF FORM

One of the best approaches to understanding a novel is to establish first of all what *kind* of novel one is reading. How does it resemble other novels like it? Northrop Frye separated kinds of literature into four modes — romance, irony, tragedy, and comedy — and listed the conventions, the recurring patterns, in each of them. Romances, for example, usually contain heroes and heroines who have more power and status than ordinary people. They sometimes even have magic of some sort on their side. Another pattern in romances is the journey or quest, often a descent to an underworld or adventures through dangerous terrain, in search of something of extreme value — from a device to save the world, to new knowledge about human nature, or even the way to spiritual redemption. The settings of romances usually involve nature in springtime, which corresponds to the youth and loveliness of the central characters. Good and evil are clearly distinguishable from one another and evil is finally defeated so that the lovers live happily in some timeless world — either a perfect garden or a heavenly city. In either case, the social order and the personal order are integrated into a complete harmony.

A work of art in the mode of irony contains the exact opposite patterns to that of romance. The characters in it are often confused or weaker in power and status than ordinary people so they find it difficult to be heroic or even to succeed in small ways. The setting is usually winter or a bleak landscape without growth or sustenance. Good and evil are not clearly distinguishable from each other so that the characters are confused and misled. It is a world in which the

34

individual feels profound alienation from nature and the social order, and there seems to be no possibility for integration. The ending of such works is often sad or open, and the reader is left with ambiguity, irony, and a rather pessimistic view of human nature and human aspirations. We often refer to such works as "realistic" though they can also take the form of satire or dystopias.[1]

In *The Loved and the Lost*, we find examples of both the patterns of romance and the patterns of irony. Jim McAlpine is on a quest of a sort since he has left his job teaching history at the University of Toronto because his superiors did not like his methods. He has come to Montreal to write "an uncensored column in the *Sun* on world affairs" (2) after attracting the publisher's attention with his article entitled "The Independent Man." These details connect him to the knight alone, determined, independent in the world, searching for his dream. His introduction to the rich and powerful Carvers who own the *Sun* (!) and who live on the mountain in Montreal, places him initially close to his childhood dream to be accepted and comfortable in his ideal world. He will join all those who have more power and status than ordinary people. His quest for class and prestige takes a curious turn after he falls in love with Peggy Sanderson. She lives in "the city below." His pursuit of her increasingly takes the form of a trip into the dark underworld of nightclubs, shadows, and her cellar room. At one point he loses sight of Peggy and imagines "all the whitened figures crossing the street down there loomed up like ghosts wandering in the world of the dead into which she had vanished, and his heart pounded, and he was sick with anxiety" (200). The hero of a romance usually goes through some sickness and danger before winning his goal, but his return to health signals his rejuvenation or even his salvation. Here, however, there is no such signal given. Jim is also challenged the way the quester is to make a very difficult decision, even to rescue his beloved from the powers of evil. Jim fails in his quest for both his love and his ambitions.

In fact, the novel reveals more patterns of irony than of romance. There is, for example, no clear line distinguishing good from evil in this story. Everyone fails in one way or another. It is a winter-time world in which integration of individual desires and the social order seems to be impossible. The coming of a spring-like morning at the end of the story does not presage new life or redemption the way it usually does in romance. Instead, it only seems to make Jim feel the panic and loss of his chance for a meaningful life. The ending is open and ambiguous. Has Jim learned something valuable about himself that will place him on a better road to self-fulfilment? Is he now more alienated and lost than ever because he does not even have his naïve optimism to help him survive? Does the little church he is looking for even exist anymore?

We noticed in the previous section that some critics objected to the combination of the two modes of romance and irony because they seem incompatible. The assumptions behind such criticism may be too prescriptive. A fairer question is what effect does this combination create? Evidently Callaghan must have been after this effect or he would not have been satisfied enough with the novel to send it off for publication. Obviously the conventions of romance set up certain expectations in readers used to fairy tales, adventures and love stories. Callaghan moves us in the direction of romance and then dashes our expectations. The pathos of Peggy's murder is amplified by the shock. Jim's disappointment in himself wrenches the reader's attention to issues that have been half buried in the telling of the events. What would *anyone* do with a Peggy Sanderson? Can such a person survive? Can society survive if we were all like her? Does love demand loyalty to such wilful behaviour? Does living with values outside those of our social laws and mores *necessarily* mean isolation, persecution and even death? Milton Wilson's reaction is perhaps the best one to start with:

> Callaghan's uneasy mixture of parable and case-history, of hagiology and sociology, has always threatened to fall apart, even in his best novels; still before they are over, I have usually ceased to worry about their possible short-comings as critiques of convict rehabilitation or race relations or the stratification of Montreal society; the documentary has been swallowed up in the moral fable. (Conron 1975, 81)

Parables are close in form to folktales, fables, and myths in that the events are narrated in a pared down fashion so as to isolate a moral lesson, implicitly or explicitly, or at least to get the reader thinking about the moral truths suggested by the events and the characters' reaction to them. The impulse behind a parable is didactic. Surely, Callaghan wants his readers to ponder the answers to the questions asked above and whatever other questions come to mind. At times he seems to direct our answers himself by intervening in the story in his own voice, as we shall see. At other times, however, he seems to confuse the issues by redirecting our attention or deflecting our expectations. There has always been some debate as to whether or not Callaghan is writing pure parables or something closer to realistic social criticism. Barry Cameron, who believes Callaghan is a didactic writer who uses parables as illustrations of moral truths, tries to have it both ways:

> Specifically, a parable is a brief concrete analogue of a general ethical situation, and in the extended form used by Callaghan in his novels it is usually expanded to include some complexity of incident and distinctiveness of characterization as well as a fullness of setting, but the ethical analogy that is the animating principle of the parable remains clearly discernible. (Staines 70)

Conron and others argue that "Callaghan's intention is aesthetic, not moral, namely to share with perceptive readers an intimate and personal experience drawn from his imaginative observation of the human condition" (Staines 98). He draws on what he knows of life and modern learning not to present an orthodox Christian or religious view of life so much as to present the "truth" of the experience of living life. The form of the novel, then, is social criticism and the style is realism.[2]

The use of conventions of the mode of romance, coupled with the moral and ethical issues in the novel, push the reader in the direction of parable. The use of the conventions of the mode of irony, coupled with social criticism (issues of racism, class, justice), push the reader in the direction of psychological and social realism — the aesthetic vision. Surely the form of this novel embraces elements of all four kinds of story-telling: romance, irony, parable, social criticism. They can be imagined as four transparencies each with a different design placed one over the other to produce complex and interesting effects. Whether or not they all blend together seamlessly, whether or not the combination "works," is ultimately a matter of taste. For some readers it does; others may be bothered by it for their own reasons. One thing is certain: the final design was what Callaghan was after because he continued to write in this form for sixty years.

THE MATTER OF STYLE

How well the kinds of story-telling are integrated will depend to a great extent on the style of writing Callaghan uses. Style, for purposes of this discussion, is limited to the choice and arrangement of the words on the page. It involves such things as diction, syntax, sentence types, tropes, symbolism, dialogue, and the like. Ultimately, a writer's style determines the tone of the narration, so the two elements cannot be discussed in isolation. Callaghan modified his usual style for *The Loved and the Lost* to make it more 'literary' — i.e. the sentences are a little more embellished and the whole work is more consciously and tightly structured. The best way to understand how the style works is to examine a section of the prose closely. The first two paragraphs of the novel are as good a place to start as any:

> Joseph Carver, the publisher of the Montreal *Sun*, lived on the mountain. Nearly all the rich families in Montreal lived on the mountain. It was always there to make them feel secure. At night it rose against the sky like a dark protective barrier behind a shimmering curtain of lights surmounted by a gleaming cross. In the daytime, if you walked east or west along St. Catherine or Dorchester Street, it might be screened momentarily by tall buildings, but when you came to a side street there it was looming up like a great jagged brown hedge. Storms came up over the mountain, and the thunder clapped against it . . .
>
> But the mountain is on the island in the river; so the river is always there too, and boat whistles echo all night long against the mountain. From the slope where Mr. Carver lived you could look down over the church steeples and monastery towers of the old French city spreading eastward from the harbour to the gleaming river. Those who wanted things to remain as they were liked the mountain. Those who wanted a change preferred the broad flowing river. But no one could forget either of them. (1)

Most of the sentences are simple or compound in construction. A slightly more complicated fifth sentence describes walking around the city; the more complex construction is intended to catch the activity of ambling around the streets. The repetition of simple and compound sentences carries a number of effects. There is, first of all, a documentary, or journalistic, quality to the prose. It is as though we are reading a list of facts being reported by an objective observer. Callaghan's early newspaper experience is credited for this style. The simplicity of the prose not only creates distance between reader and text, it also suggests something of a children's story; it has a 'once upon a time' quality to it, suitable for fables, legends, parables and other kinds of moral tales.[3] Callaghan runs the risk of a monotony of tone using this kind of syntax so exclusively, but it seems to be a risk he is willing to take in order to get the right combination of realism and parable working simultaneously.

The two paragraphs also contrast with each other: one deals with the mountain and the other describes the river. The mountain is associated with security and the river with change. The two paragraphs establish a spatial contrast (above and below, ascent and descent) which will be repeated throughout the novel in a variety of ways. It is usually inelegant to start a sentence with the word "But," however, Callaghan starts the second paragraph with this word because it serves to qualify all those strong, "secure" assertions in the first paragraph. The same sentence reminds us that "the river is *always there too*" [my italics] — the paradox that change is a permanent condition. The search for security and permanence in the face of uncertainty and change, of course, is an underlying theme of the novel. The last sentence reminds us that we have to consider *both* mountain and river, security and change: "But [again!] no one could forget either of them." We will recognize the irony in that last sentence only when we come to the end of the novel and discover that Jim's mistake is that he forgot the river, so to speak. It is also important to note that both mountain and river are described in terms of both dark and light: "a dark protective barrier against a shimmering curtain of lights," "gleaming cross," "all night," "gleaming river." These simple details of setting establish this theme from the beginning in a very self-conscious way. Some critics feel that the analogies are too obviously imposed, making the symbolism stand out too much, but one can argue that in moral tales they have to stand out. At the same time, the details are faithful to the city of Montreal making it recognizable and establishing a mood just right for the events in the story.

There are other significant images salted into this opening passage which tie in closely with details of the action as it unfolds. Callaghan tried to avoid ornamentation in his prose. When he used it, it usually was for a very calculated effect. Here we find two similes in the first paragraph. One compares the mountain to "a great jagged brown hedge," anticipating the experience described by Jim later in the same chapter when he watches the Havelock house from behind a thick hedge (9). The other simile also establishes an image pattern that is repeated throughout the novel: "At night it rose against the sky like a dark protective barrier behind a shimmering curtain of lights surmounted by a gleaming cross." The simile (mountain = dark barrier) makes the Carver's world sinister and hints at where the narrator stands. The "gleaming cross" completes the light-dark image pattern that recurs in the text while at the same time introducing a set of Christian symbols that will also turn up from time to time in the story. (The sentence could use some careful editing for punctuation. Callaghan seems to have disliked commas as unnecessary ornamentation, but the flow of his sentences is often confusing without them.) Finally, we note the thunder "clapping against" the mountain and the sounds of whistles "echo[ing] all night long against" it, concrete images suggesting that the mountain is continually attacked and anticipating the central conflict in the events of the story and in Peggy and Jim McAlpine themselves. In fact, the weather and peoples' reactions to it is mentioned on practically every page.

Almost any passage in the story can be analyzed in this way. There is a very tight interlocking of symbols, diction, analogies, and images throughout the text, as we shall see. There are relatively few of these patterns, but they are used over and over causing some readers to object to the monotony of their repetition. The effect, however, is that they both evoke and unify the reader's moral responses to the events and the characters as things get more and more complicated. The antithetical sets of images (dark–light, above–below, mountain–river, black–white, church–leopard, inside–outside, hedge–beach, sun–moon, boots–hats) at first set up a dualism in the world circumscribed by the novel. Gradually each image seems to change places with its opposite reminding us that we cannot forget either side. Whether we are to conclude from this that Callaghan was a philosophical monist, as Larry McDonald insists (Staines 78), confused, as David Helwig believes (Staines 104), an unorthodox Christian humanist, or simply an artist holding all opposites in tension, as Conron asserts (Staines 98), depends upon one's interpretation of the novel as a whole. It is clear, however, that the style of the writing indicates that Callaghan knew what he was about every step of the way. The words are obviously very carefully chosen and arranged. In order to complete an interpretation, however, all the other elements of the novel have to be assessed in light of the stylistic features.

The style of the prose determines the tone of the work. Here the tone seems to be a combination of two things: a direct narration by a simple storyteller whose vocabulary and syntax is simple and informal for the most part, and another kind of narration containing hidden subtleties and nuances suggested by literary allusions and symbols contained in dialogue and setting. Consequently, the reader is invited to be emotionally drawn into the story and also invited to be intellectually alert at the same time. The tone is both engaging and objective, casual and urgent, informal in the text and formal in the subtext. In order to pin it down any further, we have to pay close attention to Callaghan's use of narrative point of view and his use of irony.

POINT OF VIEW AND IRONY

Before attempting to interpret the novel, it is necessary to have a clear understanding of its narrative point of view — who is telling the story or whose perspective dominates the story? If we go back to those opening paragraphs, we notice that we seem to be listening to an objective narrator describing the landscape. He is omniscient and uses the third person pronoun to establish that he is outside the action looking in. He also comments on what he describes: "It was always there . . . ," or, "Those who wanted things to remain as they were . . . ." There is a slight complication in that the passage introduces Joseph Carver and could be taken to be a description of Montreal from his perspective. It is not exactly clear whether or not what follows is Carver's opinion or the "objective" narrator's commentary. The "you could look down . . ." section gives us Carver's perspective; however, the following "editorial" sentences are not likely his. It is fair to say that the rest of the novel depends for its effects on this delicate shifting of narrative point of view. In fact, there are four kinds of narrative statements in the text: those clearly belonging to a neutral narrator who is simply filling in details, recording conversation, or pushing the action along (exposition); those clearly describing a particular character's experiences, thoughts, memories, perspective, from inside that character; those which give us the narrator's opinion explicitly; and those ambiguous passages which can be taken to belong to *either* the character or implicitly to the narrator, or *to both simultaneously*. Because the shifts among these kinds of statements is subtle, occurring sometimes in the same paragraph or even in the same sentence, we are always unconsciously aware of the presence of the outside narrator. The effect is that we keep our distance at all times from all of the characters no matter how intense their troubles or their feelings. The reader is encouraged *not* to identify with the characters as much as to ponder along with them, sometimes sympathetically, sometimes with pity, often with a certain amount of disgust. Different readers will attach more weight to each of these responses, perhaps accounting for the variety of interpretations of the text. One must assume that this effect is calculated by Callaghan — that this is exactly what he wants to happen. It is not simply a clumsy mistake.

The first chapter opens up with Joseph Carver's perspective, as we have seen. A little later, we shift over to Catherine Carver's perspective (3). Then we are back with Joseph for a short spell until we get to a point where the narrator and his two characters all seem to be blended together (5). On the next page, we shift to Jim McAlpine as he tells Catherine about his childhood experience, but half-way through that monologue Callaghan switches to indirect discourse so that he seems to be taking over from Jim. The chapter ends with a shift back to a neutral recording of a conversation between the Carvers. What Callaghan does, in other words, is to establish the convention that the reader is allowed to follow any character at any time. Then he uses this convention very sparingly but at crucial times throughout the novel. Of the twenty-nine chapters which follow, roughly seventeen belong to Jim alone. The others contain the inner reactions of Catherine, Wolgast, Foley, Peggy, Bouchard, and a whole chapter is given to Mrs. Agnew when she finds Peggy's body. In fact, the opening and closing few chapters provide a kind of envelope around Jim — a casing made up of "outside" characters' perspectives. The centre chapters stay close to Jim's perspective to be sure, but they, too, are not always limited to his reactions alone. Peggy, Wagstaffe, and Wolgast are given their own first person narrations to draw us closer to them. Callaghan insists we keep some distance from Jim. His most important memory, along with many of his interior monologues are narrated in indirect speech — a technique which discourages intimacy between reader and character. When he experiences his most intensely emotional crises during the hockey game, and at the end of the story, we are abruptly moved into Catherine's mind in chapters 21, 27, and in parts of 3, 14, and 28. In other chapters that seem to belong to Jim alone, there are still a few sentences here and there which direct us to other characters' inner responses even for just a flash of time. This is not to be a story simply about a hero in search of himself, victimized by the moral confusion all around him. It is also a story about a man who makes a fool of himself as a result of his own infatuation, racism, and ambition. Callaghan does not want us to know for sure where one story ends and the other begins. Hence he never allows us to "live inside of" Jim exclusively, or for too long, lest we forget to make our own judgements of everything going on around him.

Of the four kinds of narrative statements listed above, the first two (neutral narration and interior monologue) are relatively easy to identify and can be found even in the opening paragraphs. The third kind of narrative statement comes directly from the omniscient narrator telling us things or giving us opinions of his own (editorial narration). To what extent is our judgement prescribed by this omniscient narrator? As we have seen, some of the critics resented Callaghan's "interference" because they felt he confused matters more than he should have. In point of fact, this narrator surfaces fewer than a dozen times. As we have seen, those two "editorial" statements in the first two paragraphs probably belong to him. At the beginning of chapter eleven, he draws our attention to the things Jim does not notice about himself (80). Twice in chapter thirteen the narrator steps in, once to comment on how a couple looked in the club (106), and another time to point out how "McAlpine forgot his own sensible unprejudiced attitude toward all coloured people and his rational good will . . ." (108). Later, we read: "His surprise and his joy blinded him. And he did not realize she had kept her own opinion of the trumpet player" (137). Jim had asked Peggy if she was in love with Ronnie Wilson, and she had angrily rebuked him by saying he really wanted to know whether or not she had slept with him. The conversation was redirected, and the narrator draws to our attention that Peggy never did give him a straight answer. At another crucial point in the lovers' relationship we read:

> His humiliation blinded him to the meaning of her anger. He did not realize that his kindness and love had broken through the passive indifference she had shown that day when he had tried to kiss her, and that now she had to resist and struggle not only against him, but against herself. He knew he had hurt her, but he did not see that he had done it by arousing her own desire. He did not see that, if she yielded, she yielded also to him her view of her life and of herself. He was also too bewildered to realize that she was now afraid of his gentle concern and his passion, and that it tormented her more now than any pressure all the others could bring to bear against her. (152)

Clearly, Callaghan intrudes here to point out Jim's blindness, and Peggy's own dilemma, in order to indicate that neither of these two characters understands the implications of their complicated relationship. Note, too, that the words "blinded," "he did not see" (twice), "bewildered," are unequivocal, calculated to distance the reader from Jim and even to portray him as rather insensitive for a lover. It should be remembered too that Peggy's inner reactions are recorded ("arousing her own desire," "she was now afraid. . . . it tormented her. . . ."), along with her inner conflict of which she is probably not consciously aware ("she yielded also to him her view of her life and of herself"). Callaghan again uses the same language about Jim on page 161 ("he failed to see. . . ."), but these are among the relatively few times we find the narrator leading our judgement. The intention is clear: to encourage us to keep our distance from McAlpine (and at times from Peggy) in order to understand the nature of his character and the dimensions of his errors. They are not calculated to draw any firm conclusions, only to define the psychological and emotional subtleties of the problem. At one point the narrator intrudes simply to speculate. Jim has convinced Peggy to let him use her apartment, and she jokes about her need for him. What follows must be the narrator's voice:

> But what she had just said surprised her. Maybe she suddenly remembered Malone barging in with her. Maybe she had some

sudden doubt of herself and a remembered awareness that she liked having him around and in touch with her. "Well, if it's so important to you," she said reluctantly, "if you wouldn't bother me, if you'd get out when I came home —" (156)

The speculation in the repeated "maybe" could be Jim's or even Peggy's speculation about herself, but there is no reason to believe it is. The passage belongs more to the narrator, but its possible ambiguity brings us to the fourth kind of narrative statement in the text.

The narrative technique that Callaghan uses far more often is called free indirect discourse, or "style indirect libre," a technique perfected by the nineteenth century French novelist Gustave Flaubert. (There is a passing reference to his *Madame Bovary* on page 140.) It can be found in the fourth kind of statement the narrator makes — a statement that could belong solely to the character's thoughts, insights, state of mind and spirit, *or* it could belong by implication to the narrator, *or* to both at the same time. The use of this device produces an irony of tone and often an irony of situation not only in the sense that we are distanced from the protagonist (it most often applies to Jim), but also in the sense that moral judgements are difficult to locate.[4] Is Jim right here? Does the narrator agree with this, or is he just suggesting possibilities? Are we in fact to discount this insight as another example of Jim's hopeless blindness? The usual way to get this effect is simply to omit the words "he thought" or variations of that phrase ("he saw," "he worried," "he anguished" etc.). Another way that Callaghan creates the same effect is by listing a series of rhetorical questions. We find one or both of these strategies used on virtually every page dealing with Jim; clearly, all of the passages cannot be identified or analyzed here. A few important examples will express the idea.

At one point Jim wrestles with himself about telling Catherine of his interest in Peggy just after she has criticized herself for trying to change people:

But he felt uncomfortable that she could acknowledge with such innocent good will the flaw in her nature that made her want to tamper with other people's lives. He had been trying to believe he intended to tell her about Peggy; now he had found an excuse for a secret withdrawal: if he mentioned Peggy, she would see her simply as a picture on a wall that had to be straightened; she would want to straighten him out too, in his attitude toward the girl. By rejecting and pitying Catherine's possessiveness he could believe he was free from the same trait himself. (82)

The first sentence describes his feeling. The second sentence takes a step back from his internal state and describes his psychological conflict. The words "trying to believe" and "found an excuse" are not words he would use to describe himself, so they indicate the presence of the narrator and imply a criticism of his character. His "excuses" to himself indicate his resentment at being "put in order" by someone else, thus placing him in Peggy's ideological camp. The last sentence of the passage becomes the crux of the issue. The context suggests that Jim may have this insight into the workings of his own psychology since the previous sentences describe his response to Catherine. If so, he is to be admired for his candidness. However, if he is not thinking this to himself ("he could believe. . . ."), then the sentence has to be read as the narrator's ironic comment on Jim's self-deception — that he is as culpable as Catherine but, unlike her, he cannot admit it to himself. If this is the case, Jim is to be rejected and pitied, not Catherine. The irony, in any case, will apply when we see how Jim tries to organize everything in Peggy's life. The ambiguity we experience when we try to locate the origin of the sentiment leads to an irony of tone which is subtle. This irony provides a subtext that pervades the whole novel.

At the end of chapter seventeen, just after Jim has persuaded Peggy to allow him to use her apartment for his work, we read:

"Thanks, Peggy," he said, quietly exultant. He had wormed his way into the room, he would worm his way into her life and into her heart and take her life into his. (156)

Are we to assume that McAlpine would characterize his own cunning as "worming his way"? Perhaps. We have to remember, though, that he is the writer who has made his reputation by writing about "The Independent Man" (2); the language used to describe his actions is indeed ironic and must belong more to the narrator than to Jim even if it is not clear who is making this observation. In the final betrayal scene, we read:

"I understand," she said gently. There was a silence. With a compassionate understanding, she was letting him keep his belief in his good faith.

But she had a new calmness. She raised her head with a shy dignity. The loneliness in her steady eyes and the strange calmness revealed that she knew he had betrayed himself and her, and that at last she was left alone.

In the moment's silence he tried to grasp what was revealed in her eyes; he almost felt it, but it was lost to him in the anguish of deeper uncertainty about her acceptance of the honesty of his belief that he did not want to cheapen her. (222)

Again, this passage could be read as taking place entirely inside of Jim's consciousness. Does the third sentence refer to Jim's awareness of Peggy's silent forgiveness? Is it rather Peggy's inner awareness of her own loving forgiveness, since the paragraph starts out with her voice? Is it the objective narrator telling us something that neither character really "knows"? A reading which makes the whole passage Jim's would make the second paragraph of the passage a devastating critique of Jim since it would indicate that he knows all along he "betrayed himself and her." This reading is thrown into some confusion by the next sentence which suggests that he does not understand what is in Peggy's look. If this is the case, are we to understand that the second paragraph describes the omniscient narrator's perception? Is it Peggy's point of view we are privy to here? Both? In any event, "it was lost to him," we are told by the outside narrator, before we re-enter his doubting mind in the last part of the final sentence. That last sentence also suggests that his reluctance "to cheapen her" is an honest motive on his part. The ambiguity (some might say confusion) of the point of view in this passage deepens the moral dilemma for the two characters and inhibits the reader from drawing simple conclusions. Yet the passage is crucial for any interpretation of Jim's character, his failure, Peggy's status as victim, martyr, or tragic hero.

The final page of the novel depicts Jim alone with his thoughts, but again, the indirect discourse creates some ambiguity about who is judging whom:

Yes, what they say is unimportant, forever unimportant to me, he thought. I know what happened, Peggy. I know why you're gone. In a moment of jealous doubt his faith in her had weakened, he had lost his view of her, and so she had vanished. She had vanished off the earth. And now he was alone. (257)

The first part of the passage is clearly a description of Jim's inner resolve. The latter half is more ambiguous. Does Jim believe he had "a moment of jealous doubt"? If he does, is he right or is this the result of guilt and self-doubt? Does Callaghan want us to accept Jim's self-incrimination or are we supposed to see in it a good deal of ironic self delusion? A paragraph later we read: "He hurried along eagerly, believing he had found a way to hold on to Peggy forever." The word "believing" seems to come from the narrator and could connote more self-deception in Jim. The romanticism of the final phrase could also suggest an ironic sub-text, especially in the light of his solution — to find the little church. He is still looking for it when the novel ends. This complicated use of indirect discourse draws us closer to McAlpine and moves us away from him, sometimes by turns, sometimes simultaneously, so that we are never very sure where the firm moral ground is located. The controlling centre of awareness slips around until the reader is left baffled and very much on his or her own. This is a calculated effect. Brandon Conron summed up what is involved at the Callaghan Symposium:

> As Milton Wilson has noted, "The special talent of Morley Callaghan is to tell us everything and yet keep us in the dark about what really matters. He makes us misjudge and rejudge and misjudge his characters over and over again; we end up no longer capable of judgement, but not yet capable of faith." Callaghan himself has consistently maintained that it is an artistic weakness to give "the reader a chance at too quick a recognition" or to put "the writer and the reader in a comfortable relationship . . . meeting his reader and reviewers on their terms, and it should always be the other way around." (Staines 97)

Obviously, Callaghan's use of narrative point of view has its part to play in creating this uncomfortable relationship between writer and reader, and between reader and characters.

Closely related to the use of point of view is the use of various kinds of irony. Callaghan liked to quote the American critic Ivor Winters who said Callaghan's stories contained "chemically pure" irony

(Wayne 17). What he probably meant was that irony can be found in dialogue, situations, characters' judgements, even in images and symbols, throughout the novels. It is not the kind of irony that draws attention to itself for satiric or humorous purposes. It can hardly be detected the first time through the story. The second reading, however, reveals that it is in *The Loved and the Lost*.

An example from the first few pages indicates its presence. McAlpine is introduced as a man in possession of a "straightforward and poised" manner and "quiet self-confidence" (3), along with "a quiet faith in himself" and "an exciting strength of character" (5). Catherine, on the other hand, fears "if she revealed it [ardor] she would suffer again the bewildering ache of her husband's resentful withdrawal" (3). By the end of the novel, McAlpine is anything but self-confident or strong, and Catherine has been shattered once again after doing just what she feared to do. The irony of the Carvers' reaction to Jim is emphasized a few pages later when Joseph Carver refers to Jim's "absolute faith in his own judgement" and his "unshakable belief in what he thinks he sees" (11). (The word "thinks" contains an irony inside.) This kind of verbal play in the dialogue is Callaghan's favourite device for undercutting his characters and for foreshadowing both events and moral crises. When Jim first meets Carver, to cite a typical example, he tells Jim about his difficulty with his fat employee, Walters, who refused to follow the tomato diet suggested to him. In the same conversation Jim mentions that in his article he insisted,

"[T]hat a man can make adventurous choices in his own life, particularly in his difficult relationships. It might be necessary for him to say to hell with the job."
"H'm-m. Absolute independence, eh?"
"The trick would be never to knuckle under in the face of a difficult relationship. Do you see?" (30)

As it turns out, the irony in this dialogue is thick. Jim does not realize that he will be in the very situation he theorized about and that he will fail in his most important relationships. The "Do you see?" has immediate and long term resonances. Carver, too, misinterprets Jim to mean he should fire Walters. Immediately, Jim thinks about Peggy in the context of this conversation but he does not understand why he feels unhappy (31). A little later, Chuck Foley warns Jim to beware of Carver because "he reaches right into [employees'] lives till he owns them" (74). Jim will attempt to do the same thing to Peggy when he takes over her apartment. The same idea is expressed ironically when Carver complains in one breath about a son who has taken over his father's estate, and in another breath he expresses admiration for painters because they "can always put people and things in the right place in the pattern" (82). Catherine admits she "must be a painter." This conversation not only underscores the notions of possession for power, and the security found in predictable patterns, in a number of later conversations and internal monologues, but also ironically anticipates the drawings Jim does of both Catherine and Peggy, both of which eventually give him away to the police and to the Carvers.

There are other cogent examples of this use of irony in dialogue in which characters either say much more than they realize, or say things that will turn out to be relevant later on in the story. At a party, a drunken Jim overhears the words "stupid self-deception" and asks himself if they apply to him. The narrator intervenes, clumsily this time: "But he refused to deal with his own question. It was easier to ask, What if Peggy, too, had been deceiving herself, not only about her life but about her true feeling for me?" (121). Jim may be evading an important issue here, but later on the question does become a relevant one. Its relevance is anticipated by the rest of the conversation about self-deceiving idealists who have "no prudence — ready to hurt anybody who got in her way" (122). Mr. Carver ends the dialogue with the warning: "It's fine to be independent, Jim, but don't be fool-hardy" (123). The warning *is* heeded by Jim but leads to his admitted failure. It is *not* heeded by Peggy and leads to her destruction. Carver has no idea how important his words are. There are any number of examples of this technique of placing ironic statements in the dialogue. Note how the lovers' final encounter contains a double irony:

"Oh, Jim!" she said, tightening her arm around him impulsively. "Don't ever leave me, will you?"
"Never?"
"No, never."
"May I stay here tonight?" (219)

He does leave her. His second question throws into doubt his love of her in the first place. He does not stay the night and she is killed as a result. Ironies layer and complicate the apparently simple scene.

Besides planting ironic phrases in the dialogue and in the diction (verbal irony), Callaghan also sets up situations for ironic effect (situational irony). Near the beginning of the novel, Jim is "irritated by [Catherine's] resentment of his friendship with Foley" (23), but he never seems to credit Peggy's irritation over his resentment of her friends. On another occasion, he walks with Peggy and neither knows nor cares where he is going; in fact he gets "mixed up" (36), anticipating his moral muddle later on, and his final lost stroll. Likewise, he kisses her when she does not welcome it (42) and refuses to kiss her when she does. The same ironies inform scenes of Jim stopped in doorways. (Jim on thresholds has its symbolic weight too.) At the end of chapter six, for example, Peggy suggests that Jim leave her place, but he lingers, not wanting to go (48). At the end of chapter eight, Jim at a night club is in exactly the same position, "hating to go; he felt a compulsion to wait, a bewildering sense of urgency that he should wait and not leave her alone in there" (66). At the end of the story, of course, he leaves when he could have stayed. Another example involves Jim losing his hat at the hockey game in the mob confusion over an injustice. From that point on, Jim wears a hat borrowed from Joseph Carver, ironically signalling his real allegiance even though he has convinced himself he is loyal to Peggy. When he finally gets to Peggy's place after the mob scene in the bar, the first thing he mentions is getting back his hat and coat (214). The irony is subtle, but his anxiety over the hat that identifies him with the world of the Carvers anticipates his abdication of loyalty to Peggy. In a final scene with Catherine, Jim explains his relationship with Peggy including his final decision to leave her for the night. Catherine slaps his face, not because of his disloyalty to herself but because of his betrayal of Peggy. Jim does not understand the difference (252). Situation after situation is mined for its ironic content.

There is also irony in the many judgements expressed by the various characters throughout the novel — a variation on situational irony. Most of these opinions revolve around the innocence, wilfulness, or imprudence of Peggy Sanderson's social behaviour. It becomes clear that the various judgements about Peggy reveal more about the speakers' anxieties, prejudices, desires, and blindness than they reveal about Peggy. The Carvers simply want to maintain standards of taste and class. Malone wants to be assured that he is as sexually acceptable as any Negro. Milton Rogers is sure that Peggy is ignorant when it comes to economics and dismisses her as promiscuous. Wagstaffe feels that she is undiscriminating and phoney, a naïve trouble-maker. Professor Fielding remembers her as a mediocre featherbrain. Henry Jackson thinks of her as a modern Saint Joan. Mrs. Wilson sees her as a home wrecker, while Mrs. Agnew and the people in the factory respond to her open friendliness. Wolgast simply thinks of her as bad for business and an insult to his dignity and status. All of the various opinions challenge Jim to make his own judgement and to have faith in it. Indirectly they challenge the reader to do the same thing. Instead, these opinions all seem to sow seeds of doubt and jealousy. The narrator never contradicts any of the opinions by demonstrating that Peggy does not fit the description, nor does he tell us directly that she is blameless. In fact we see the results of her presence — dissension, anger, frustration, and finally, violence. None of the communities in which she is involved seems to benefit from her presence. If Callaghan uses irony in dialogue and narrative technique to maintain separation between the reader and Jim, he uses irony of situation and event to maintain a distance between reader and Peggy too.

Irony has a number of applications and definitions as we have discussed it so far. It is a "mode," or form, holding conventions of realism and satire. It also creates a distancing effect between the reader and the characters in the story as seen in Callaghan's techniques of narrative point of view. Irony, more particularly, means saying one thing and meaning just the opposite. The opinions expressed by the characters, including the presentation of Jim's thoughts, along with the placing of ambiguous words and phrases in the text, add up to this kind of dramatic and verbal irony. As Wayne Booth has demonstrated in *A Rhetoric of Irony*, the reader goes through four steps when confronted with irony: 1. we reject literal meanings; 2. we try out alternative meanings; 3. we make a decision about the author's unspoken intentions and beliefs; 4. we reconstruct what the author really means according to our decision about his beliefs or feelings. If we feel sure that we are not invited further to reconstruct other possible meanings, then the irony is "stable" — we are sure we know where the author stands. If, however, it seems impossible to tell where the author stands, or if ironies seem to duplicate themselves so that there is no possibility for reconstructing meaning securely, the result is "unstable irony." Booth asserts that works can be divided in one or another kind:

In one kind, all or most of the ironies are resolved into relatively secure moral or philosophical perceptions or truths; in the other, all truths are dissolved in an ironic mist. (151)

If Callaghan is designing a parable, he depends upon stable irony. We should be confident that we can reconstruct the way he really understands his characters and their world as a reflection of actual experience. The style and form of the work suggest that he is describing our real, contemporary world, while at the same time fitting this description inside a roughly sketched parable. Interpretation of the text will entail reconstructing the narrator's beliefs or feelings even though we sense ambiguities and unstable ironies. The decision as to whether the ironies altogether add up to stable ones or unstable ones will determine the attitude we finally take to the novel. What clues are there in the story that help us to decide what Callaghan really means or where he wants us to stand at the end of the story? To answer that question, we will have to examine the novel's structure, settings, characters, image patterns, and themes to see if there is unity of vision underneath the details of action.

STRUCTURING THE STORY

Of all of Callaghan's novels, *The Loved and the Lost* is his most unified. He seems to have gone to great lengths to structure the story into a seamless whole. He has used suspense, symmetry of characters, settings and scenes, literary allusions, and a limited number of image patterns to hold his story together. The reader who may feel uncomfortable with the complexities and ambiguities created by ironies will nevertheless feel that the world circumscribed by the novel is a consistent and highly patterned one. There is a built-in unity to the novel by virtue of the fact that we follow Jim McAlpine's experiences, largely limited to his perceptions of events, for the majority of the story. However, since irony is at work even in the author's treatment of his protagonist, he had to use other techniques to give the story its unity and to give the vision behind the novel its integrity.

Suspense

The reader rides along on the tracks of character development and suspense. Momentum is established by a series of simple questions. Will Jim McAlpine realize his ambitions in the face of the challenge to his values represented by his attraction to Peggy? This is the strongest thread holding the story together. The second thread involves the fate of Peggy: what will happen to her, and eventually, who killed her? Callaghan sows seeds of suspense and suspicion in practically every chapter. The very first time Jim meets Peggy, for example, there is a hint of the violence which will surround her: Foley tells him that a man at the office named Fred Lally is "making a play for her" and if he gets out of hand "he'll get pushed in the nose" (19–20). The repeated references to impending storms, Peggy's lack of hat and boots (reinforcing our sense of her vulnerability), her entranced interest in the leopard, all help to foreshadow her rape and murder. We are also reminded of her indiscriminate friendliness by Mrs. Agnew who admires how much company Peggy has in her flat (38), and by Jim's observation that the bell with Peggy's name under it "had been smudged by so many fingers it was almost indecipherable" (83). (This is what literally happens to her name as the novel progresses.) Jim meets strangers visiting her place — Cowboy Lehman (84) and a shadowy intruder he thinks he recognizes before the man escapes (199). Peggy reports that she was followed home by a man with a wooden leg, and that she has been walked home by Papa Francoeur and by an infatuated eighteen-year-old named Willie Foy. Further, Jim is also witness to explicit threats to her safety. Walter Malone raised his hand to strike her on one occasion (132) and angrily declares he "will lay her" (148) on another. Henry Jackson punches her in the eye, and Claude Gagnon volunteers to "hold her while he booted her in the pants" (146). Lily Wilson also threatens Peggy's life (194), and Wolgast tells Jim that he will cut her face with a broken bottle if she brings another negro into his bar (173). The Negroes are equal threats: Ronnie Wilson cannot go home because he stabbed a man to death in Memphis; Elston Wagstaffe does not want Peggy in his club; Joe Thomas tells stories about "how a good-natured human being like himself can suddenly go berserk" (134). Even Chuck Foley and Milton Rogers are hostile towards her. Callaghan lines up a whole series of suspects as the story progresses. When Peggy is finally raped and strangled, it is Jim who is the primary suspect and it is Jim who insists he killed her. We never do find out who actually ended her life. That is the final irony since Callaghan seems to insist that a great many people, even society itself, must share the blame. How much Peggy herself is to blame becomes a moot point.

Symmetry

Another element unifying the novel can be found in its patterns of symmetry. Characters, scenes, and settings are contrasted and balanced against each other so that the reader is encouraged to think of the issues in the novel, at least initially, as "either/or" propositions. The symmetry seems to suggest a dialectic in the novel. As the story progresses, the balancing elements compound, and although the aesthetic harmony is enhanced by this technique, thematic clarity begins to break down. The dialectic seems to dissolve. Consequently, we always feel we are in the hands of a writer who knows exactly where he is at any given instant in the novel; we just lose track of what to make of what is going on. We have to assume that this is a calculated effect, i.e. give Callaghan the benefit of the doubt and then ask how are our responses coloured by this structural device?

Characters seem to be contrasted with each other in pairs. Catherine is tall, twenty-seven, handsome, rich, blue-eyed, reserved, sophisticated, outwardly assertive and inwardly fearful of relationships with men. She takes Jim seriously and is attracted to him immediately. Peggy has "a childlike prettiness" (17), is poor, blond, hazel-eyed, short, not at all afraid of relationships with men, impulsive, passive, without "much style" but "completely feminine" (19), and in possession of a "strange kind of stillness" (17) and a "charming innocence" (18, 19). She does not take Jim seriously and is not attracted to him at first. The two women seem, at least superficially, to represent two different value systems, and Jim has to choose between them. Other characters seem to be paired: Wolgast is a Polish Jew who wants to protect his club; Elton Wagstaffe is a Negro bandleader who also wants to protect his club. The editorial writer, Walter Malone, feels he is in exile from Paris and is a violent man. Ronnie Wilson is in exile from the U.S. for a violent attack on a man. Henry Jackson, the lame commercial artist and dramatist, is a foil for Jim. Both of these intellectual artists are attracted to Peggy. Both lose faith in her. Jackson seems designed to symbolize the spiritual cripple Jim can become. Minor characters also emphasize various themes: Peggy's father is a hypocritical clergyman and Jim imagines the priest at the hockey game would be no more sincere (180). There are a number of women who also form patterns. Peggy was raised by a pious Mrs. Mason who is the opposite of Mrs. Agnew. Jim, whose mother also died when he was young, is drawn to the figures of mothers with children, as well as to the figures of old women, on a number of occasions.

Parallel scenes also balance and contrast each other. Jim's childhood memory of being snubbed by the Havelocks (9) is parallelled by Peggy's childhood memory of the Johnson family (46) and her story about the time she tried to get Sophie Johnson a job in the hospital in Hamilton (93). Wolgast's childhood recollection of the white horse (169), Catherine's memory of fending off an aggressive lover on the beach when she was eighteen (237) is balanced by Peggy's memory of a college boyfriend's gaze making her feel beautiful (137). Even Henry Jackson's history of illness when he was a child and his mother read to him ("Those sick periods had shaped his whole life. . . .") (140) all contribute to the Freudian notion that individual lives are determined to some extent by powerful early experiences. Jim also tells Foley about an incident in Paris during the war when he unexpectedly came upon a little circus (77); a memory offset by Wagstaffe who, on another occasion, recalls a racist incident at a rich white man's home in Paris (101). Each of the latter recollections offers an exactly opposite insight into Peggy Sanderson's behaviour. Other parallel scenes involve numerous ones of Jim walking with various characters — to stores with each of the women, for example; Jim's attempts to kiss Catherine and later Peggy and being rebuffed by both; Jim drawing each woman's portrait; scenes of violence at a hockey game and then at the bar; Jim denying his relationship with Peggy to Catherine and later to Angela Murdock; and scenes at the Earbenders Club where Jim is being told how to understand Peggy's motivation. Each scene, by recalling and reflecting the others, becomes a piece in an increasingly complicated puzzle which both confuses and compels the reader.

Settings are also balanced and contrasted. As we have seen already, the mountain and the river are said to represent stability and change, rich and poor, ambition and oppression, upper class and lower class. The mountain is also dark or black as contrasted with the white snow all over the city. The two clubs, Wolgast's Earbenders Club in the Chalet Bar and Wagstaffe's Café St. Antoine, turn out to be very similar kinds of place, each turning Peggy away for the same reasons. The circus setting in Jim's lovely Paris memory is the antidote to the Montreal Forum where a mob takes over the officiating of the hockey game.

The weather, too, is described on almost every page. Snow, frost, wind, and mud seem to be everywhere, thus establishing a mood of depression and caution. People are continually described as huddling against the cold or protecting themselves from sleet and storm. Icicles are singled out at times of danger throughout the story. This use of setting helps to reinforce the feeling of the isolation and vulnerability of the characters. The weather also takes on symbolic significance. The night of the hockey game riot is "the coldest night of the year" and McAlpine asks, "How cold can it get around here?" (180), referring in his own mind to the treatment that Peggy receives from society in general. The landscape may even suggest the fallen state of mankind in archetypal terms — the king of life, growth and regeneration is missing or dead. In this context, sunshine is often used ironically. It is associated with corporate power — the Sun Life Building, the newspaper called *The Sun* — as well as with Jim's renewed ambitions and the restoration of order after Peggy's death. Peggy and Jim express a preference for hot weather, and all the best memories recollect summer.

The hedge around the Havelock home in Jim's childhood trauma is used to describe the barrier of the mountain a number of times, just as the details of Wolgast's story intrude into Jim's vision when he imagines a white horse trampling Peggy on the side of the mountain (256). Other details of setting such as the cross on the mountain, the little church, the leopard in the store, the repeated references to white snow, will be examined in a section on imagery and symbolism.

Setting also refers to social setting, and Callaghan uses Montreal's cosmopolitanism to advantage. He tries to include various ethnic groups: the Polish Jew, Wolgast; Negroes such as Wagstaffe and the Wilsons; Irishmen Foley, Doyle and Malone; the English Carvers, Fielding and Jackson; Gagnon and Bouchard, the French Canadians; the Jewish gynaecologist named Sol Bloom; the Scots as represented by Mrs. Agnew. Callaghan makes clear his intention to represent a world social order when he describes the crowd at the Forum:

> There they were, citizens of the second biggest French-speaking city in the world, their faces rising row on row, French faces, American faces, Canadian faces, Jewish faces, all yelling in a grand chorus; they had found a way of sitting together, yelling together, living together, too, and though Milton Rogers could shrug and say, "Our society stinks," even he had his place in this House of All Nations, such as the one they had in Paris, and liked it. (178)

Ironically, as it turns out, Peggy came to Montreal because of its mix of people — her romantic dream of brotherhood.

Allusions

Suspense, and symmetry of characters, scenes and settings, help to unify the story. Literary allusions also suggest ways of thinking about its wholeness as well as implying that its experiences cut across time and place to describe common human experiences. There are only a few explicit literary allusions in the novel. Others are implicit or covert. The most obvious reference is to the myth of Orpheus and Eurydice:

> "He makes speeches like music," Gagnon said finally. "Beautiful speeches in a pleasant tone. The right kind of music for Peggy. You follow me? There she is, lost in the dark underworld. Montreal's Plutonian shore. Like Eurydice. Remember? Remember the lady? Remember? How did Eurydice die?"
> "Bitten by a snake," Foley said.
> "And certainly our little Peggy has been badly bitten."
> "So McAlpine becomes her Orpheus."
> "Ah, yes, there you are. Her Orpheus."
> "Orpheus McAlpine!" (148–49)

This exchange is in response to McAlpine's reasoned defence of Peggy's interest in Negroes. In Greek mythology, Orpheus was rumoured to have come from the north or from Mount Olympus, son of the muse Calliope and the god of music and the sun, Apollo. Apollo is also often considered a god of order, reason, the aesthetic harmony of art. Orpheus was mortal; nevertheless he played and sang so beautifully that he tamed wild animals, the rivers stayed their courses, and rocks and trees came sliding down mountains. He descended to the underworld of Hades to recover his wife Eurydice after she had been bitten in the foot by a snake as she was fleeing from the shepherd Aristaeus. He pleaded with the gods of the underworld to give her back her life for the sake of their love. He was told that he could lead her back to the upper world only if he did not look back to make sure she was following him. At the threshold of the two worlds, he did look back and Eurydice faded away. Orpheus's motive for looking back is not clear. He may have simply wanted to assure himself she was still there (lack of faith in the gods, or in her?), or it could have been an impatient anticipation of her return generated by his love for her. His anguish was so great that he refused to have anything more to do with women and sublimated all his grief into his music. Thracian women who tried to attract him eventually became incensed at his aloofness, tore him to pieces, and threw his head in the river Hebrus. Some versions say that his head was later found and it delivered oracles. In the sixth century BC, a cult was founded after Orpheus. The Orphics were among the first to assert the doctrine that a heaven existed above for the blessed after they were released from matter as we know it and the bondage of the world.

Clearly this myth has been used to advantage by Callaghan. Jim McAlpine can speak persuasively (his music), is obsessed with order (Apollonian), charms those around him (even Henry Jackson), is artistic, and, as his name suggests, he aspires to the mountaintop where he feels he belongs. Peggy is not that charmed by Jim's conversation at first, and this frustrates him: ". . . her irritating serenity made him feel he wasn't really interesting her. People had always told him he talked beautifully. Everybody said so" (37). He charms her in time, falls in love with her, and moves into her home to work. It is his insecurity and lack of faith in Peggy, according to one reading of the novel, that results in her death. Jim seems to worry about Peggy's feet a good deal — a possible allusion to Eurydice's wounding by the snake. However, the snake episode is a little awkward to fit into the context of the story. The conventional reading would be to assume that the snake is the evil that killed her. Yet we are encouraged to think of Peggy as existing in an underworld from the beginning of the story, before she is killed. If this is the case, the snake could be interpreted as something evil in herself or in her environment (". . . Peggy has been badly bitten").

This is a possible interpretation since Callaghan goes out of his way to exploit his setting of Montreal for its vertical spaces to indicate that Peggy is in the underworld. Peggy lives in a dark basement flat. Jim is continually travelling down from the mountain to see her. ("At midnight McAlpine came down Mountain Street. . . ." opens chapter seven, to cite only one example among many.) He finds himself, at one point, at the bottom of "the steepest flight of stairs he had ever seen" (189). When she tells him she works at the factory, he says, "Are you sure it's safe for you down there?" (89). Her flat is often associated with darkness and chaos, and she is seen in the clubs sitting in dark corners. Watching from above, Jim sees Peggy leave for work, and he imagines all the people "down there" as "ghosts wandering in the world of the dead into which she had vanished" (200).

The slap he receives from Catherine at the end of the novel is an echo of Orpheus being torn apart by the Thracian women. The Orphic cult, which eventually influenced Christianity to separate matter and spirit, is relevant in that it established a dualism between "worlds." This idea of two separate planes of existence also informs one possible theme of the novel: the notion that genuine love and spiritual values cannot exist in the fallen world — that there is no place for the innocent and passionate saint in the real world either of Westmount or St. Antoine Street.

Another literary allusion is contained in the title. Section 27, lines 15–16 of Alfred Lord Tennyson's "In Memoriam" contains the lines: " 'Tis better to have loved and lost / Than never to have loved at all." The meaning of these lines — that although a loved one may die, the experience of love transcends death — is altered by Callaghan and made abstract. "The loved" may refer to all those to whom Peggy offers her altruistic view of humanity, but they refuse her and destroy her. It may refer specifically to Jim, the loved one, who cannot recognize Peggy's and Catherine's love for him, but once Peggy and Catherine are gone, he is forced to rearrange his priorities because he now knows the true value of love. "The lost" may refer to the alienated people of the post-war years when values have been so confused that love cannot grow in them. These people wander aimlessly, unable to identify the love that alone gives human lives meaning and dignity. The word "lost" is used on three occasions. Jim's first article is about the "lost men of Europe, the mass of men who were driven by some death wish to surrender their own identity and become anonymous parts of a big machine: he intended to make the point by devoting each column to one character, one lost man" (160). He seems to fail to see the application of his concept to himself; he wanders lost at the end of the novel. Catherine, too, thinks of all the things she has lost: "All the lost things of her life would fill her thoughts on those nights when it snowed . . ." (185). Later Jim spots a man lurking around Peggy's place, but before he can identify him, he "was lost among other snow-covered figures" (199). It seems to be a world of the lost. It could be argued that, paradoxically, it is because Jim loves Peggy that she is lost.

One other explicit allusion in the novel is to George Bernard Shaw's play *Saint Joan*. When the play is mentioned in a conversation meant to tease Henry Jackson, his response is that Jim could never understand a girl like Joan of Arc. In a rather clumsy interior monologue, Callaghan has Jim reflect on the similarities between Joan and Peggy:

He waited jealously for Jackson to reveal that he, being close to Peggy, was aware that she, like Joan, lived and acted by her own secret intuitions. Joan had shattered her world, and Peggy shattered people too. Not only Malone, but Mrs. Murdock; even Foley. She would shatter all the people who lived on the mountain and the people who prayed on the mountain. Joan had to die, he thought with a sharp pang, simply because she was what she was. (144)

The reference places Peggy in the tradition of Christian martyrs and saints who fought for Christianity without compromise. George Bernard Shaw's interpretation of Joan was that she was a force that moves human civilization forward but is a scapegoat for progress since she is so ahead of her time. Peggy refers to herself as a scapegoat a few days before she is killed (196). Are we to think of Peggy in unequivocal terms because of these references? We have to keep in mind that it is Jim, not Callaghan, who makes the connections between the two women. Jim even realizes that Jackson was not referring to Peggy at all. To what extent are we to assume that Callaghan is behind the assessment of Peggy as holding "secret intuitions" and shattering worlds and people? To what extent is he, himself, putting lights around this passage flashing "author's message"? It is by no means clear that this is the case since, as we have seen, Callaghan makes us keep our distance from Jim and his judgements. It could be simply another attempt at suspense by foreshadowing Peggy's death ("there were many others like Malone, who would destroy her" [144]). It could be a way of guiding our response to what Peggy is really all about despite what others say about her. If so, it is still only one more opinion among many.

There are also a number of incidents in the text which are not literary allusions so much as echoes of incidents in the New Testament so that they function the same way as literary allusions: they point our response in a particular direction. The "gleaming cross" in the opening paragraph, and "the little old church, half Gothic and half Romanesque, but light and simple in balance" (36), which Peggy shows Jim, and which he seeks at the end of the novel, suggest that Christian values play an important part in our understanding of the story. The cross represents the sacrificial love of Christ to save mankind from original sin (sometimes referred to as the human condition), and the old church could suggest the Christian religion before it became too much a part of the political order of worldly societies. (A number of churches are listed when Jim looks for this old one the first time, but he rejects them since they seem too grand or simply tourist attractions [85].) Peggy could be placed under the banner of the true Christian church as opposed to that represented by her father or the priests.

There are, in fact, other events which reinforce this idea. Her room resembles "a monastic cell" (38) when Jim goes there for the first time, and she when she lies on the bed, she "crossed her legs at the ankles" (39) as in a crucifix. She also offers him grapes on that occasion, a possible allusion to the wine of sacrifice. Saints' names are kept in front of the reader at all times since the street names and places in Quebec are used liberally: Saints Catherine, Antoine, Agathe, Patrick, Henri, Joan, Thérèse, is a short list. All were martyred.

Other allusions to Christianity can be found in Jim's denial of

Peggy three times: to Catherine in refusing to tell her about Peggy (24, 82); to Mrs. Murdock ("But his denial of Peggy had left him stricken with remorse." [128]); and to Mrs. Wilson (". . . because you're her man.' 'Oh, no!,' he said." [194]). Peggy is murdered at three in the morning, just when the cock crew after St. Peter's denial of Christ. In fact, the mystical number three surrounds Peggy. Jim has to "ring three times" for her (71); there are "three bells for the three apartments" (83) where she lives; she had "a fever that lasted three days" (93) before her "whirling-away feeling" (91), echoing a death and resurrection motif. The morning of her death "three giant icicles had formed on the steps and were dripping over the basement entrance to Peggy's apartment" (224), a possible veiled reminder of the three crosses on Calvary. The first time she laughs, she cries out "Oh, Lord, I'm getting a stitch in my side!" (91) recalling Christ's crucifixion. Like Mary, she wears blue and white on many occasions, and she lives on Crescent Street. In the Roman Catholic tradition, Mary is very often depicted dressed in white and blue and standing on the crescent moon. Peggy is also referred to as "kissing the leper" (97), and giving off a "big church glow" (103). Jim is obsessed with whether or not she is a virgin. On one occasion, Jim kneels in front of her to take off her boots, a gesture reminiscent of similar gestures in the New Testament, as is the time she washes Jim's face (217). During the fight in the bar, Peggy is pelted with garbage and jeered at when she leaves the club, again reminiscent of the scourging of Christ (212). That Catherine makes "washing motions with her hands" (239) after the murder, associates her with Pontius Pilate and may implicate her along with the rest. Even the statement that "All [Joseph Carver] missed was his rose garden" (2) might be read for its Christian references. These allusions may be judged to be too subtle or arcane, but like Joyce, Callaghan used these kinds of associations in all of his previous works. After all, he inherited his icons from his Roman Catholic training and he consistently attempted to show how Christian thought was lived in ordinary contemporary lives. New Testament images and events can be seen to form a sub-text in this novel, although they are hidden and subtle — perhaps too subtle for some to allow them any final significance. The question is: to what extent does the religious content demand more attention than the classical allusions (Carver and Jim seem to discuss Horace, Catullus, Plato and the like whenever they meet), or the Freudian or Marxist explanations? The reader must either identify the notes of emphasis, or search for whatever balance of forces is available in the text.

Imagery

Along with the unifying devices just discussed, there is an open weave of other kinds of recurring images and symbols holding the novel together. The most obvious set of images can be found in Callaghan's use of colours. There are remarkably few colours mentioned; however, those that are used are found everywhere. The most common colours, of course, are white and black. Along with these basic colours are a handful of others. The clothes that the characters wear are white, black, blue, brown (or copper or tan), and in a few limited cases, grey, and green. A certain pattern emerges from these colours. The businessmen and the general population always wear brown and sometimes grey; these colours seems to represent the status quo. Even the portrait of the Murdock patriarch is painted "in browns and blacks and burnt sienna tones" (122). Henry Jackson wears brown and grey (141); Wilson is first seen in a light brown suit (62) and usually wears camel or tan colours (224); a stockbroker wears a grey outfit (202); Malone is a "grey ham" (52); an Englishwoman has a brown coat (70), and so does a French Canadian at the hockey game (177), and a Negro in the final brawl (210); and the Negro women seem only to wear copper coloured dresses (105, 193, 205). The buildings are grey (27, 254–55) as is the sky very often. Catherine usually wears brown fur coats and hats, and as a child wore a brown suit to a birthday party and found three other girls had also worn brown suits (185), reinforcing the association of the colour brown and conformism. Although Catherine is the most colourful dresser in the novel (114, 176), at the end she cannot decide between a brown dress and a blue one (236). She walks around the house in a white slip until she has decided to turn in her evidence against Jim at which time she chooses the brown dress (239).

Blue is a colour that belongs to Peggy and the poor. Jock Johnson wore blue overalls and a blue sweater in Peggy's recollection of him on the beach (45). An elevator man has a blue uniform, and Peggy wears the blue overalls that the people in the factory wear. She also has a blue kimono (149), a blue skirt (61), a dark blue jacket (95), wore a blue birthday dress to her party when she was a child (47), is compared to a bluejay (76), and Jim at one point tells her that her black eye will turn "all blue" (150). Jim's affiliation with Peggy is suggested by his blue overcoat when he is introduced (2), and by his blue suits (136, 243). He and Peggy seek the little church in "a bluish light" (36), and Bouchard's understanding of Peggy is signalled by his blue tie (239). Green is mentioned only a few times in connection with Mrs. Agnew (37–38) (who also has a blue dressing gown [71]), Peggy's summer dress (137), and Catherine at the Ritz Carleton (114). Green seems to be a colour of hope for love in each of the contexts in which it is mentioned: Mrs. Agnew expects her friend from St. Agathe; Peggy remembers a lover when she was at university; and Catherine wears green when she meets with Jim.

The two colours used most often in the text are white and black. They form a backdrop for all the action and they are consistently ambivalent. The constant mention of snowflakes, frost, clouds, smoke, or white light on almost every page, along with policemen in white (33), white streets (16), singers in white or silver dresses (61, 77, 206), white boots on the girls (59), make the canvas upon which the story is set a white world. If Callaghan were to be compared to any Canadian painter, it would have to be David Milne who chose one or two predominant colours and then added only a few more, very lightly here and there, in order to suggest that one could look *through* the patterns on the canvas to what was hinted at beyond what we see. White is associated with sterility and death very often (Peggy is dead white on page 227), but it is also associated with innocence and spiritual resurrection as in the Easter liturgy and lilies. These two associations are appropriate for the story since we are dealing with the possibility of spiritual resurrection in a "dead" postwar city. Callaghan adds black to his palette by giving Peggy black skirts, a black dress (136, 159, 227), along with her white blouses (61, 106, 159, 195, 206, 227). The mountains are black at night, as are table tops (99), Jim's memory of the hedge of his childhood, the Negroes, and the dimly lit clubs and hallways. Black, too, usually signifies death, but we have to remember that Peggy's love for Blacks is behind her serenity and pain. Sometimes a pink glow from neon lights gives the scene a surreal feeling (56, 66, 213), but once again, Callaghan turns the colour positive when the sky turns pink after Peggy's death (256).

Other images which recur with amazing frequency are also connected to clothes: hats and boots. Hats are mentioned at least forty times in the novel. Jim meets a man at the beginning of the novel who is identified only by his hat — Persian lamb (13–14). He tells Jim that when he can afford such a hat, he will know he is successful. Hats signal social identity, prestige and success. Of course they also protect against cold and storms. When Rogers tells Jim that Peggy is seeing a violent Negro, a number of images are coordinated: "Too shocked to speak, McAlpine grabbed at the rim of his Homburg as the wind whipped at it, and the snow blowing in . . ." (110). Wind and snow anticipate the social and psychological storms initiated by Peggy; Jim has to keep his hat against the assault. His typical gesture is to grab for his hat (69, 110, 174, 198). Peggy says she never wears a hat (17, 34), which emphasizes her vulnerability, her disdain for social identification, and her lack of common sense, all at once. Snow "formed a crown" (20) on the hats of Foley and Jim, and Catherine's hats are fur, again associating hats and the corporate world of success, riches, and class. Catherine, Mrs. Agnew and others shop for hats (60), and the people at the Hockey game are described in terms of the hats they wear (177–78). Jim also finds the snow forming "a halo on his Homburg" (33), indicating the potential for grace he is offered, but at the hockey game, when a crowd becomes a mob by discarding their hats, Jim loses his hat ("What am I going to do for a hat?" [183]), and borrows a Homburg from Mr. Carver: "The men in the black Homburgs can all wear each other's hats. Keep it, my boy" (188). He forgets it during the brawl when he struggles to save Peggy, but worries about it when he gets to her place (214), and retrieves it after she is killed. It is the first thing Mr. Carver worries about when it becomes clear that Jim is a suspect in the murder case (240). Significantly, Jim gives the hat back to Mr. Carver after he has acknowledged his part in Peggy's death (244).

Footwear, feet, and footprints form another rich image cluster in the text. Peggy is first seen without protective footwear and her footprints being covered with snow seem to mesmerize Jim (20, 31). He notices her footprints often — likely a reminder of the Eurydice archetype. When Jim notices Catherine's "handsome leather snow boots," he thinks of Peggy's exposure (23); likewise, when Carver's power over Walters is made clear to him — "an unfamiliar world of humiliating bondages" (31) — he remembers Peggy's footprints. Jim's desire to protect Peggy first takes an unconscious form: he decides to buy her a pair of brown leather boots. He also feels he has to protect himself against Peggy, indicated by the fact that he forgets to take his galoshes off after he has been shocked by Rogers's description of Peggy (111). Again, when Peggy has been assaulted by Malone, she keeps her boots on in her flat (133, 135). Jim kneels down to help her take them off — his first genuine gesture of love. When Jim visits Peggy just after she has been assaulted by Henry Jackson, she greets him in her bare feet "which were so surprisingly small that he couldn't take his eyes off them" [sic] (150). In their final encounter, it is Peggy who is worried about Jim's wet shoes and he spends his time in his stocking feet (216–17) thus imitating her and implying symbolically that he shares the vulnerability of love. The only detail Callaghan inserts when Jim is leaving her is that he put on his shoes (222).

It is ironic that Peggy should find work in a shoe polish and lighter fluid factory. She also has a certain affinity for crippled men. When she walked home with Jock Johnson, he stubbed his toe on a stone and she bandaged it for him (45). Her boyfriend is Henry Jackson, who wears a "special shoe with a built-up heel" on his left foot (141). Jim thinks that Jackson's whole attraction for Peggy is that he reminds her of the Johnson boy (142). Cowboy Lehman walks with "shuffling uneven footsteps" (83) when he visits Peggy. An old man who jokes with Peggy in a bar limps toward the stairs (61). She is followed home by "a man with a wooden leg," and Papa Francoeur explains to Peggy that he cannot seduce her because "his legs were always swollen" (89) from walking up the factory stairs. All we ever know about the man who killed her was that he is heavy-set and that he walks with "a slow heavy step" (234). There is something vaguely Freudian about the way these images work in the story. The need to protect, to rebel, to sympathize, even sexual impotence, are all possible motives which seem to be hidden in the gestures and circumstances. Once again, as in the use of Christian iconography, Callaghan employs his images of clothes not so much to drive home one particular paradigm to prescribe our interpretation (propaganda), but to suggest that there are a number of congruent possibilities in explaining behaviour.

Any interpretation of the novel will also have to take into account the many references to words connoting light — sun, glow, shine, illuminate, burn, gleam, and the like. The sun is often a symbol of order, harmony, intellect, and power. In mythology it is represented by the god Apollo, father of Orpheus in some versions of his story.

Carver, of course, owns the newspaper called *The Sun*, "as influential as any newspaper in the country" (27). The sun is "bright" and "hard," and its warmth is "liberating" (232) after Peggy is murdered. It melts the snow as Jim looks for the church at the end of the novel. The lighted tower of the Sun Life Building is mentioned as a powerful negative presence on a few occasions, almost as an antidote to the gleaming cross on the top of the mountain. Significantly, it blocks out the moon (56) and "loomed up against the darkening sky" (174). Other references to the sun indicate that it is also a positive image. They occur exclusively in the context of youthful memories of love or beauty. Peggy recalls seeing Jock in the sunlight (44), and Jim dreams of having Peggy "walk with him in the sun's glare" (69) when he was at university. Wolgast, too, remembers his childhood in the sun (168–69). Both Peggy and Jim prefer hot weather. In this context, Montreal in winter is reminiscent of Dante's version of hell as a bitterly cold place.

The moon in mythology is feminine, associated with goddesses of virginity and the night world of sexuality, insanity, beauty, and fertility. Jim is excluded from the Havelock house under the moon-light, a light which "was driving the dog crazy" (10); it is "only a pale flicker" (56) behind the Sun Life Building; it "glinted on the steeple of the stone church" (149) after Jim is compared to Orpheus; it is a dominant part of Catherine's memory of a first sexual encounter from which she fled (237), and of her decision to expose Jim (238). Peggy lives on Crescent Street. Generally, then, the sun image accompanies corporate, social or intellectual power, or lost beauty. The moon seems to signal a faint presence of some feminine grace.

Words denoting light are used all through this night-time story. Callaghan emphasizes his underworld setting by pointing out the necessity of lights as well as indicating how often areas are dimly lit (38, 51, 157, 160, 168, 198). He has a fondness for the word "gleam" which he uses to describe the cross and the river in the opening paragraphs as well as the hedge (9), the mountain (58), light from the sky reflected on buildings (118), streets (242) and heads (126, 209) including Peggy's hair when she is dead (242). This word describes light as reflected back from surfaces — the light of the world of concrete reality. Related words such as sparkled, shimmered, shine, glittered, glistened, also connote the idea of harsh, false, reflected light in a world that is both white and dark. Wet snowflakes "glittered and

shone" in a "glistening winter-white brilliance" (59), or the "whole
rich mountain glistened" in a bright morning light (256). Street lights
"shimmered" (199) as does the city on the mountain (1). The lights
on the mountain also "glitter" (223–24), as do Bouchard's eyes glitter
with "intellectual sympathy" (249). Malone's eyes have a "glazed
sparkle" when he is about to attack Peggy (132), and Wolgast's bald
head "is shining brightly" (139) as is Fielding's (127). The word
"light" is itself used over twenty-five times, usually to describe light
reflected from paintings (61, 81, 191), streets (56, 130), windows and
doors (56, 119, 149, 254), or faces in shadow. As mentioned earlier,
the light is often pink in contrast to the "brilliant white light" at the
little circus Jim visited in the City of Light (77). The word is also used
in the metaphorical sense of putting people "in a certain light."

There is another kind of light described in the novel in a recurring
image. Light seen in its most positive sense is captured by the word
"glow." Here the idea is that the source of the light is inside; it is not
a mere reflection of light, but a container and generator of it. Virtually
every time the word is used, it connotes love or generosity of spirit.
Catherine impresses Jim with "the glow of her generosity" (5) when
she is falling in love with him and later when she is at ease with him
(82). Peggy is described as giving a "big church glow" (103) to
everyone, and possessing an "indescribable glowing freshness"
(195). Her life has a "disturbing glow of a poetry in it" (119), and Jim
dreams of bringing her to a place "where she would glow with a
singleness of love which would bring her happiness and not destruction" (109). When Jim feels particularly close to Catherine, the whole
city seems to glow (116), and in his debates with Peggy "his eyes
glowed, he spoke out of his heart, and though it was supposed to be
a rational discussion it was really his argument of love" (191).
Catherine's eyes "glow with hatred" (242) when she learns of Jim's
relationship with Peggy, and hearing about Peggy, "glowing ardently
. . . she identified herself with the other girl" (250). The image is used
to suggest a quality of relationship as well as a quality of spiritual
experience in an individual. Jim is pulled into this source of light in
the women, and he seems to recognize its value intuitively. In fact,
this word seems to be one of the few obviously value-laden words
in the text, and it may be a hint as to how we are to find the moral
centre of the novel. In his other works, Callaghan used the word
"eagerness" to suggest this same tendency to see the world positively

— an intuition of inner harmony and grace in all of creation, particularly in people. It suggests a kind of innocence which is not simple ignorance, but something intuitive, beyond rational understanding. It could be a quality of both perception and understanding — a generosity of spirit that is based in the Christian idea of love. In the post-war world, it is almost always doomed.

The word "whirl" is used often enough to attract attention to itself also. It has both positive and negative uses just as the other images do. The snow "whirls" around McAlpine (26, 36) as does smoke from a passing train (57), indicating that he feels lost. When he struggles to rescue Peggy from the bar-room brawl, he "whirls" (212), and his thoughts "whirl" later when he tries to figure out whether or not he should spend the night with her (220, 222). The more positive connotation of the word has to do with Peggy's description of her "whirling-away feeling" (91). When she discovers her father's hypocrisy, she decides to leave him and she feels "a lightness of spirit; I felt myself whirling away from things he had wanted, whirling in an entirely different direction" (94).

This image of circles is paired with its opposite: images of stability found in the words "order" (4, 157, 158), "pattern" (63, 76, 82, 136, 137, 179), "web" and "netting" (116). This need for order and stability is not seen as necessarily destructive or even artificial. At the hockey game, all order breaks down and the result is a very real danger. The purely aesthetic value of order can be found in the way the players pass ("What a pretty pattern! It's just like the ballet, isn't it?") or in a painting (82). People seem to make patterns quite naturally with the idle movements of a fork on a tablecloth (76), or with ones shoes on the floor (136). Jim feels compelled to organize Peggy's clothes in her bureau (157) not just because he is compulsive, but also because he wants to protect her from the dangerous chaos that ensues when order breaks down as it does at the game and at the bar. McAlpine knows about the necessity of order but he is fascinated by the independence of Peggy especially since it seems to be based on a genuine sense of personal integrity.

Symbols

There are just a few symbols in the story. Most of them are explained by Jim McAlpine in what seems to be his role as occasional (albeit erratic) stand-in for the omniscient narrator. The carved leopard which Peggy shows to Jim fascinates her with its fierceness and power (35). The ceiling light shines "on her wet fair hair" just as it lights up her hair when her corpse is discovered by Mrs. Agnew (237). Later, Jim interprets her fascination with the leopard as a "gentle innocence . . . attracted perversely to violence, like a temperament seeking its opposite" (112). In a drunken stupor at the Murdock's party, Jim senses the danger Peggy is in from the society around her (123), and when he sees her black eye, he interprets it as "a mark of wildness on her; it was a glimpse of a strange mixture of peace and wildness . . ." (151). No doubt we are supposed to accept his interpretation of the symbol. Peggy does attract violent reactions, and we cannot discount the possibility that she finds this exciting. However, it is also possible that she is transfixed by the evil around her the way its prey is transfixed by a snake.

The church is a more enigmatic symbol. Jim experiences "an idle, gentle interlude" and a "vast tranquillity" (36) before her sees the church. He does not know where he is going and he does not care. The episode takes place in "bluish light." The whole atmosphere is one of suspension of ordinary reality and concerns. The little church is "half Gothic and half Romanesque, but light and simple in balance." The most important part of the experience is Jim's comparison of the church and Peggy's face "on which snowflakes glistened and melted, making her blink her eyes. He looked again at the church and then at her face. Her shoulders were white, his own arms were white, and the slanting snow whirled around them. Feeling wonderfully lighthearted he started to laugh" (36–37). The church suggests early, simple Christian religion; the white snow implies innocence and purity of feeling; the words "whirl" and "wonderfully lighthearted" emphasize the spiritual nature of Jim's experience as well as the simplicity and purity of his vision. After looking at the Carver's new Renoir painting of a girl at a piano, and subsequently failing to locate Peggy, Jim goes looking for the church again but cannot find it. At the end of the novel, the church remains elusive, but it is clear that Jim is searching for the same clarity of vision he had with Peggy when he saw it the first time. This feeling of pure worth may have its religious dimension, but it is also an aesthetic and emotional experience rooted in Jim's need for his romantic ideal. Callaghan lets the description of the symbol suggest a number of facets to a spiritual experience — emotional, psychological, aesthetic, spiritual. It has been argued that the church does not suggest a religious experience at all since neither of them goes into the church, nor does it signify a Christian value to Peggy's attitude towards others since she does not seem to be impressed at all by what the church stands for. The important point here is that it is Jim's experience that is being described, not Peggy's. We have no indication what her reaction to the church is. In fact, her reaction is not that important. The church deeply impresses Jim and challenges his values at some profound, even unconscious, level. And it is, after all, a church rather than, say, a painting or a tree. Callaghan must have something in mind by choosing that particular image for its symbolical associations.

Wolgast's white horse symbolizes his dream of freedom and joy when he is a child (169), however, it is translated into a possession of property, social acceptance, and comfort when he finds his niche in the New World. When Jim is questioned about Peggy's murder, he says it is "about Wolgast's white horse" (244), and later he explains it was an ironic remark, presumably meaning that the innocent dream of the boy became the pernicious ambitions of the man (255). Finally, Jim imagines his own ambition as a white horse, and that all the white horses of ambitious men "storm" down the mountain to trample Peggy into the snow:

> She didn't own a white horse. She didn't want to. She didn't care. And he was beside her; but he drew back out of the way of the terrifying hoofs and they rode over her. (256)

The symbol of the horse becomes transformed from a desire to a nightmare.

There are three other interrelated symbols (perhaps too obviously imposed and explained): the hedge, the mountain, and stairways. Jim's ambition to "make the grade" (7) goes back to his experience when he was fourteen. He hid behind a dark hedge to test whether or not he counted to the rich Havelock family. When it became clear that they did not care about him at all, he decided to manage his life so that he would count to such people (112–13). The Carvers belong to the same circle. They all live in Westmount on the mountain, and Jim has come to cross the barrier of "the gleaming hedge, darker than the night" (10) to climb the mountain and join the gods of society on Parnassus (59) and to count among the people who control the *Sun*. The mountain and the hedge are usually tied together symbolically. Incidentally, the "gleam" of lights from the house is more alluring to young Jim than the moonlight on the lake or on the road (9). The lights on the mountain "gleam" along with the "gleaming cross" representing the social power of organized religion, as opposed to its original significance as the symbol of sacrificial love. Callaghan links his images and symbols together very consistently. When Jim sides with what he thinks Peggy represents, he tries to ignore the "black barrier of the mountain" (67, 149), "a rock of riches with poverty sprawling around the rock, and now a place that had inexplicably brought turmoil to his heart" (166). At other times he sees the mountain/hedge as a place to conquer (58); when he abandons Peggy to her fate, "he strode up the street, looking at the ridge of the mountain against the sky; the lights glittered on the ridge, and he seemed to be walking right against it, and it had never been so dark or so high" (223). After Peggy is murdered, "the whole rich mountain glistened" (256) in what seems to be a sinister triumph.

Connected to the symbols of mountain and hedge is the symbol of stairs. The novel seems to establish three levels: an upper level on the mountain, a lower level in the city below, and a subterranean level of subways, washrooms and basements. The stairs between levels are a kind of Jacob's ladder, and Jim is situated on these stairs very often, symbolizing his dislocation and disorientation. Of course the levels themselves reinforce the mythological foundations of the story (Orpheus descending to rescue Eurydice), but they also can imply metaphysical levels of experience thus encouraging a more "religious" interpretation of the text. In fact, there are signs that Callaghan wanted to suggest all these possibilities at once. The result could be more confusing than clarifying. The symbol is introduced in a section that depicts Jim descending Mountain Street "toward the dark railway underpass" (56) to the pink glare of the Café St. Antoine. He decides not to go in and continues down in the moonlight to other clubs before climbing the hill to the café that Peggy frequents. However, "The shabby street was cut off short, the way blocked by the enormous mountain barrier studded with gleaming lights" (58). At this point, he refuses to "climb the stairs" to the café where he might find Peggy. It seems that there are two kinds of ascent here representing two value systems: one to the top of the mountain and the other to whatever Peggy represents to him. The next day, he makes the climb up to the nightclub (the stairs are mentioned three times in half a page) (60), but he admits that he is probably "out of my depth" (64). His next climb is with Catherine up "high steps which were like a dark web against the snow" (116) leading to the Murdock residence on the mountain. At the top, they survey the whole city, and this is as intimate as Jim and Catherine ever get. Jim rejects the "disorder," the "strange chaotic experience" of Peggy's life on that occasion (118). When he denies that he knows Peggy to Angela Murdock, Jim goes "up the stairs to the big blue tiled bathroom" (128) to hide his shame. On the way home, Catherine remarks that "the best part of the evening really was when we were here on these steps" (129). The stairs at the Montreal Forum represent the same climb as the one up the mountain. Jim and Catherine look down on the game below in much the same way that Joseph Carver looks down over the city in the opening passage. At a restaurant, Jim descends to the lowest depth in the novel. His meditation in a washroom results in despair. McAlpine looks up the stairs:

> It was the steepest flight of stairs he had ever seen. If only he could climb those stairs, everything would be all right. Peggy would not get into trouble. She would quit her wandering. She would turn to him. (189)

As he drags himself up the stairs, he has "a moment of beautiful clarity" (190). He decides he can save her with his love. He cannot manage to save her during the nightclub brawl; he watches "her fair head disappeared down the stairs" (212).

There are a few very minor motifs which also recur (icicles, mothers with children, windows), but the point is that these image clusters and symbol patterns are very carefully worked into the fabric of the novel. A few critics find some of the patterns so carefully controlled that they seem imposed onto the text rather than emerging organically out of it. Callaghan obviously meant his symbols to stand out since he takes some trouble to offer possible explanations for them. He integrates others (snow, clothes, lights etc.) quite well into the telling of the story. The cumulative effect of these recurring images and symbols is to unify our sense of the world the novel builds up, unify style and themes, and fuse our impression that the story is both realistic and something like a parable with a moral vision behind it.

JIM MCALPINE AND COMPANY

The unity of the story rests on the foundation of Jim McAlpine's character development. His psychological and spiritual growth depends to a great extent on his relationships with the people around him, particularly Catherine Carver and Peggy Sanderson. The minor, more choric characters are not presented in any depth. For the most part they simply express alternative opinions about Peggy for Jim to ponder. Wagstaffe and Wolgast tell Jim enough about themselves to allow some understanding of why they think and act the way they do, but even these two characters seem to hit only one note. Many of them are suspects in Peggy's murder, as we have seen. Taken altogether, they represent forces of "society" (or better still, "societies," since there are a number of communities represented) — social pressures for conformity and security lined up against the pressures from within individuals to maintain their personal integrity. McAlpine, in his mid thirties, is challenged to sort out his values seriously, rather than simply in theory, by his relationships with two very different women. Any study of Jim's character will necessarily entail a study of Peggy Sanderson's role in the novel so the two characters will be studied together.

We are introduced to Jim McAlpine in the expository chapters through external appraisal by the Carvers. Jim's public image is that of a tall, broad-shouldered history professor in his early thirties who has just come out of the war where he served in the Navy as a lieutenant commander. He has developed good social skills, although he considers himself a failure as a professor because his superiors disapproved of his methods (4). We are not told what those methods were, but apparently we are supposed to see Jim as something of a iconoclast, or at least as an independent thinker who is no stranger to controversy. The Carvers agree that "he had a quiet faith in himself" and that "he possessed an exciting strength of character" (5). His faith and strength of character are put to the test in the rest of the novel. He attaches himself to Catherine for the first few weeks ("with still no sign of snow"), and conveys the impression that he genuinely needs her (5). Immediately we learn that his mother died when he was sixteen; that his father admired the president of a Trust Company, Mr. Havelock; that he also liked to write poetry; and that Jim resented the rich Havelock family for the way they snubbed his parents. As he tells Catherine about his childhood, "she was sure a wound was hidden under his calmness" (8). The anecdote about the Havelocks offers important insights into Jim's personality. His ambition to belong to the upper class social set is motivated by revenge, not by any ideological design or even greed. To that extent, it is not a genuine ambition since once he attains it, it will mean little or nothing to him, although he does not seem to appreciate that yet. The vengeful words he utters to their "gleaming hedge," "[j]ust wait" (10), seem to be a cry on behalf of his parents as well as the whisper of his own offended pride. He was never insulted directly or thrown out of the Havelock party; he was simply not acknowledged as anyone important in and for himself. His later interest in individualism no doubt starts here. Later we learn that he never went back to that beach but took summer jobs instead and "learned how to be alone" (68).

His childhood reaction is also significant in other ways. He does not become aggressive; he simply hides and waits to be missed. No one misses him in the least, and this is what infuriates him. In a way, he will try the same technique at the end of the novel with Peggy. In the first eleven pages, Jim's character takes on a good deal of complexity. He is seen as having "absolute faith in his own judgement —" and "an unshakeable belief in what he thinks he sees" (11) by the Carvers. However, his liberal belief in "The Independent Man" (2) seems to rest on the need to belong to the most powerful class in society and the need for a compassionate woman to support his ego. Catherine fits the bill on both counts. To put it in more Freudian terms, the death of his mother left him insecure and in need of women, while the more romantic side of his father gave him a fascination for independence and the integrity of individual conscience. His conservative clothes (14), which anticipate his compulsive need for order, are not explained except in so far as his father admired the liberal establishment and Jim wants to be recognized by them. His profession as historian coupled with his war experience can account for some of it, as well. His central dilemma is summed up in an interior monologue when he is trying to decide whether or not to continue seeing Peggy:

If he went on, he would be letting his curiosity get the better of his common sense; he would be forgetting that he had come to Montreal to take a job on the *Sun*, and if he got himself involved in a scandal Mr. Carver certainly couldn't afford to take him on. The job on the *Sun* was the kind of job he had always dreamed of. He had come to it after many years of waiting since the night on the Havelock beach when he had run along the road and then had stopped and looked back at the hedge, muttering, "Just wait!" That night, the end of his boyhood, he had lain awake for hours dreaming of making a name for himself some day so no one would ever have to ask again who he was. He had waited and had suffered many humiliations but had known the day would come when his talents would be recognized. (112)

Perhaps we should be told what the nature of those "many humiliations" was, but Callaghan does not say.

The lively and somewhat cynical Chuck Foley, who calls Jim "son" (15), seems to stand in for the more romantic side of Jim's paternal inheritance; he is the man who introduces Jim to Peggy. Previously, a rich man in a Persian lamb hat (as opposed to Jim's Black Homburg), an early choric voice of prudence and pragmatism, had warned Jim to "confine himself to girls like his own people" (14). Foley had dismissed any men in fur hats as unimportant. The snow first begins to fall when Jim meets Peggy. He is without his overshoes (15). Both images, as we have seen, foretell the turmoil and vulnerability of the two characters. Jim is charmed by this woman who "looked like a child" (16) and never wears a hat (17) or boots. To him, she also possesses a "strange kind of stillness" (17) and a "charming innocence that was his own remarkable discovery" (18). It is important to keep in mind that these qualities ascribed to Peggy are given to her not by Callaghan but by Jim. (Foley said she was "fresh as a daisy" [15] but he seems to be referring to her age more than anything else. She makes him feel young.) In fact, Peggy indicates that she is in control of men and her life from the very beginning. She does not give in to the men's pleas that she stay for another drink. She is amused by them; she says she gets Foley to buy her coffee every day. Jim, however, leaves the encounter convinced that he has "to protect the charming innocence he had discovered, but of course he had to conceal his feeling from Foley" (19). The use of indirect free style establishes irony in the phrases "he had discovered," and in the "of course." Who is saying these things? We are reminded that Jim is proud of his discovery while at the same time Callaghan emphasizes its subjectivity. Why does Jim feel that "of course" he must conceal his feelings? Is he ashamed? A Snob? Insecure? Already aware that she does not fit in with his ambitions?

Callaghan seems interested in presenting Jim's reactions to women. Joseph Carver notices that when Jim talks to Catherine, "his tone would change" (4). When Jim sees a woman flirt with two men outside a night club, he "grew more offended. His sense of order was disturbed. . . . A slim good-looking girl like that shouldn't have known them. It was all wrong" (16). *What* was wrong? Where is the disorder? He is annoyed at Peggy's independence when he first meets her (19). Why? Wandering around the St. Antoine district, Jim notices, from a distance, a Negro mother and child dancing together in a lighted window (56). Later, Jim is depicted avoiding the eyes of a garrulous old woman "with a benevolent motherly face" who tells the story of her "kindly life" to everyone (69), but whose "overflowing, possessive motherliness was oppressive" to Jim (70). On the same occasion he watches a mother in a brown coat with two children who are pretending to be doctor and patient. The boy finds a "big black mark" on the girl's tonsil, and the girl asks McAlpine to acknowledge that it is not real. He tells her it is not. What are we to make of these little vignettes? Jim notices mothers and is uncomfortable with them if he has to deal with them personally. From a distance, they are admired. The little girl cannot possibly have a real black mark. (In the Roman Catholic education of the time, original sin was usually described as a black mark.) It seems that Jim needs to believe in women as projections of his own romanticism; when the reality of their lives intrudes, he is disturbed.

There are other examples throughout the text. A charwoman at his hotel shows an interest in him and he is "distressed" by the encounter (111). Mrs. Agnew's loneliness unnerves him (157), as does Catherine's. He flees from Mrs. Wilson "before the misery of her married life could tumble down on him" (194), and he is ashamed that she has no faith in what he tells her. He denies his relationship with Peggy to her, to Mrs. Murdock, and to Catherine, almost as though he is avoiding the anger of a mother. A stout woman in green expects Jim to give her information about Peggy's murder, but he trembles and lurches against her (229). When he does confess to Catherine, and is slapped, he does not seem to understand what troubles her (252). When he is introduced to a mulatto singer whom he admired at a distance, he notices that "Without the yellow glare of the spotlight, her skin was grayer, the golden lustre of the flesh all gone" (98). When he imagines getting to know her, he thinks he would "always feel strange with her, but it would be a novel sensation." He thinks of her in romantic terms alone. His covert racism is also slightly exposed here under the guise of his curiosity about how Peggy responds to Negroes.

After his initial meeting with Peggy, he becomes obsessed with her. His "urge to protect the charming innocence he had discovered" (19) amounts to a need to protect his romantic notion of innocence and purity. Callaghan does not provide psychological analysis for his characters, but his usual strategy, probably rooted in his legal training, is to offer enough evidence to complete a psychological profile that is plausible if not absolutely conclusive. The evidence in the text indicates that part of Jim's obsession is a psychological projection onto Peggy of his own need to believe in the innocence and the integrity of the individual, perhaps a compensating gesture for what he unconsciously knows: that he is selling out his own principles and deeply felt values in order to become a member of the establishment. His romantic notion of women makes her a likely candidate since Catherine already belongs to the established order and the other women, as listed above, are too troubled or too old to qualify for this role.

The difficulty is that the opinions surrounding Peggy, as well as some of the evidence Jim is given, create serious doubts in him about the object of his projection. He cannot deal with her as an unique human being either way: she has to measure up to what he wants her to be, or alternatively, she is condemned to be what others say she is. She is probably neither, but we can never know since Jim is our major source of analysis and the minor sources of opinion are in their own ways just as suspect. It would be clearer if we had an omniscient narrator to set the record straight, but we have seen already that the narrator purposefully adopts an ambiguous and ironic position on all of the crucial issues. The effect is to make us ponder the complexities of the developing moral problems since they are linked with an individual's psychological and emotional history as well as with his or her current social condition. The free indirect style makes us keep our distance from Jim, while never allowing us to dismiss him completely. There are times when we cannot tell if the implicit judgement being make in the narrative is that of the narrator, or if it is Jim gaining insight into his own shortcomings. Consequently, we agree to wait and see.

Jim McAlpine's obsession with Peggy is obvious. After his first meeting with her, he picks up Catherine but finds himself worrying about Peggy's cold feet (23). He also resents Catherine's advice about the kinds of friends he chooses (24). Clearly, he is not that committed to the mountaintop. Catherine senses this in his restrained kiss — a clue to Jim's unconscious knowledge that he is selling out something he values in himself:

> He put his arms around her waist and he kissed her, but did not hold her hard against him. It was not a warm full kiss. . . . But her doubt showed in the way she lifted her head; he saw it, yet was afraid to hold her against him, afraid she would know his heart was not beating against hers, and know, too, that his mind was somewhere else, enchanted by a glimpse of something else. If he had only mentioned the girl it wouldn't be like this. (25)

The embrace has its metaphorical connotations, but more importantly, Jim's mind is "enchanted" by "something else" rather than by *someone* else. Peggy is already an abstraction, "the girl," a projection of a value that Jim feels the need to believe in. His next encounter with Mr. Carver, and Carver's misinterpretation of his idea of independence, which in Carver's mind becomes power over others, waters the seed of doubt Jim is growing — the nagging sensation that his ambition to join this class may be mistaken. Once again, Jim's mind jumps to Peggy when he thinks of "an unfamiliar world of humiliating bondages" (31). The pattern, the order, the system, demands giving up some of one's individuality and therefore one's freedom to be oneself. Jim feels ashamed and flees from poor Walters (32), only to start thinking again of Peggy, as the snow forms a halo on his hat.

It is at this point that he begins to think about what she represents to him: innocence or "something in her nature like an act of peace." He dismisses her as "an idle intellectual diversion" (33). He tries to place her intellectually, rather than to respond to her intuitively, impulsively, passionately, or in any other way available to him. His "retreat" (if that is what it is) into an intellectual analysis is his way of protecting himself emotionally, and holding on to his ambition. On their excursion to see the leopard and the church, however, intellect has nothing to do with his experience. The impulsive way she takes his hand makes him feel self-conscious at first, and he all but admits that he has never felt at home anywhere (35). Soon, though, he is too immersed in the emotional and aesthetic quality of the leopard and the church to think about "where he was going and he didn't care. It was just an idle, gentle interlude, and his vast tranquillity amused him." Unconsciously (or so it seems given the ambiguous nature of the narration here), he had grabs her arm to save her from the violence represented by the leopard (36). The way the church and Peggy's face make him feel ("wonderfully lighthearted") allows him to put a leopard and a church together, however irrational that may seem to him (37). Later, he is irritated by her self-possession ("serenity") because he cannot seem to impress her with his talk — his ego is offended. Orpheus is losing his power (37). He buys her grapes even though "They don't go with the snow" (37), and he accompanies her to her poorly lighted "monastic cell" in the basement on Crescent Street.

Peggy's behaviour at this point can be interpreted as naïve or as provocative, or both. She invites Jim in and lies down on her bed, "her hands clasped behind her head" (42). In the context of 1951, this is unusual behaviour for a young woman even if she is completely indifferent to the man she is with. When we read, "Her blond hair and pretty face on the pillow invited his caress. She had a voluptuous, suggestive appeal which drew him down to her," it is not clear if this is simply Jim's misinterpretation of her demeanour, or if this is the narrator's accurate description of her behaviour and she is actually inviting his sexual initiative. When he decides to kiss her and to caress her breast, he is met with a "rebuke of passive indifference" and the odd comment that he should give his repressed "sweet streak" a chance to develop (42). The "sweet streak" is presumably his penchant to be a gentleman and declare his respect for her, or she could mean some intuitive part of his nature that is "all cluttered up," but the passage is enigmatic, since we are not allowed into her mind or motives at this point. Her reaction to his sexual advances on this occasion colours his interpretation of her for the rest of the novel.

Peggy then fills in some details about her childhood. She, too, lost her mother. She was raised by a pious housekeeper and her Methodist minister father in a lonely household. Jim says, "Lonely or not, I think you would be happy" (44), reinforcing in the reader's mind his extremely romantic image of a woman he barely knows. Peggy tells him about her vision of Jock Johnson, naked in the sun on the beach, and of her new awareness "that beauty could be painful in a strange way . . ." (45). Her "secret knowledge that he was beautiful," coupled with her notions of the Johnsons' joy in life and the fact that she is accepted by them as a family member, impress upon her the pernicious nature of racial prejudice, especially when her father is reluctant to invite the Negro children to her birthday party because it would not sit well with his congregation. After fleeing from her own party and going to the Johnson home, she is dragged back by Mrs. Mason and told never to play with the Johnsons again. Her reaction is to hate herself "for growing older" and to conclude that "all the Johnsons of the world, were never to be among the invited guests wherever I went" (47). McAlpine is described as having a "light in his eyes" as he listens to this romantic story of pseudo-mystical beauty and rebellion in the cause of equality. His romantic notions of purity and innocence, of the innate goodness of human nature and liberal impulses, is turbo-charged by Peggy's story. He has the "strange desire" "to make her laugh like a happy child" (48) with a lot of talk, but she becomes bored and anxious that her date will show up while he is still around. He hangs around chattering, wanting "to defend the room" (48).

The words Callaghan uses to describe Jim's reaction all through Peggy's story are clues to the source of Jim's obsession with her. His philosophical and emotional romanticism is brought to life by his projection onto her of his need to believe in human goodness. He has managed in his life to redirect this romanticism into an ambition to be respected by the crowd for his mind — to have his life validated by money and prestige. Catherine represents the "gleam" and "glitter" of the latter; Peggy represents the "glow" of the former, no matter what else we may think of her.

That Jim decides continually to hang around her while she gets ready to go out with other men, is a measure of his obsessive foolishness. His analysis of his first encounter contains interesting psychological currents. He is "disturbed" by her story, presumably because of its Freudian possibilities, or because he cannot repress his own covert racism, though he does not think in these terms. He wants to believe she is "blameless," but he concludes that if carried too far, blamelessness "could have dreadful consequences" (48). He tries to convince himself that she is blameless, but those who do not know better might mistake her passivity as coyness and go further than he did. If so, his logic goes on, she might then have to allow "another man" (a Negro?) to have what he wants.

His growing obsession then takes the form of spying on his "blameless innocent." Foley will not help him to spy on Peggy, so he wanders around trying to get up the nerve to spy on her himself. The mountain reminds him that what he really wants is "among those who had prestige, power, and influence," but he is nevertheless drawn to the clubs by the image of Peggy in the arms of a Negro:

He turned away from the café entrance, not admitting he was afraid of what he might find in there; with a deliberate effort, using his head, he recognized rationally it was a mistake to feel so involved with her that he had to climb the stairs and suffer the embarrassment of encountering her with her friends; with an effort he broke the spell and went on home. (58)

By this time, his racism is clear. After all, what would be so awful if he did find her dancing with a Negro? Callaghan also loads the passage with value laden words: deliberate, using his head, rationally. On first reading, one feels that we are supposed to believe that he is asserting a valuable side of himself by being "rational." However, in the context of what precedes the passage, he seems to be confusing rationality with pragmatism. Again, it is unclear whether it is McAlpine alone who considers his behaviour "rational," or if Callaghan agrees with him. The narrator informs us that Jim would not admit to himself something that the narrator knows. The subtle shift in perspective that takes place with the words "deliberate effort," however, makes it possible to read the next lines as: "Jim thought he was using his head and acting rationally," with the implication that he is really simply rationalizing in his own self-interest.

A boring party in Westmount and a pleasant evening with Catherine boost his self-confidence to the point that he feels he can visit a

St. Antoine café with impunity. He cannot shake his obsession that easily, it seems. There he finds Peggy, who resents his spying on her. Possibly this is why she tells him about a time she went bowling with Wagstaffe and then had a wonderful time talking with him in her room. We cannot know if this is Peggy's way of getting rid of Jim (she dismisses him when she finishes telling her story), but it reinforces his ambivalent feelings about her:

> He wanted to believe completely in her own pure feeling. This faith in her was the illumination he had been seeking since the first time he had met her; it offered him a glimpse of the way she wanted to live, of the kind of relationship she wanted to have with all people, no matter what kind of a sacrifice might be required of her.
>
> But it couldn't persuade him that Wagstaffe, or Wilson, or their colleagues, would be content to accept only her gentle friendliness, asking nothing more of her. The utter impossibility of her attitude, its wilfulness, its lack of prudence, frightened him; but he knew that if he protested she would assume he was speaking out of the dull confinement of his own orderly university experience. (65)

To some extent, Jim has abstracted what Peggy has said to him about her views so much that he now interprets them as "her own pure feeling," willing to offer any kind of sacrifice that might be required of her. That is a long way from what she has implied about her relationships with men. Jim's anxiety is also confined to Negroes in this instance because he is sure *they* would not accept anything less than total compliance, as opposed to himself who did the gentlemanly thing. He also assumes that she will deal with every similar situation in the same way; hence, her wilfulness and imprudence. Clearly, Jim's social dilemma is mostly a pretext for a deeper psychological one. His urge to protect "her" (read *his*) pure feeling is projected onto the pure white snow that covers Montreal and is translated into his purchase of boots for her. He tries to ignore the "black barrier of the mountain" (67).

Instead of examining where Peggy fits into his own personal mythology, he thinks exclusively in social terms. He imagines his father's consternation, his navy superiors' disapproval, and the president of the university's censure of his relationship with her (72). He is evidently still impressed by figures of authority. His anxiety about social acceptance is increased by the opinions of the men around him in the Earbenders Club. Foley comes up with a preposterous theory that Peggy can no longer concentrate on work because "she's all hopped up with the dinges making passes at her and probably laying her too." He declares that her whole life is a lie in order to gain attention and approval, and that she will do anything to maintain her advantage (75). She is a "blue jay" that flies off "at crazy and unpredictable angles." Jim immediately counters with his equally preposterous theory — the possibility that she may be a saint (76). He compares the feeling he has about her to a feeling of suddenly meeting "something unexpected that's just right" like the little circus he found in Paris that was "so white and clean and fantastically surprising and so wonderfully innocent and happy" that he felt "peacefully elated" (77). He has a knack for expressing his view of Peggy as a nostalgia for childhood — a romantic preoccupation if there ever was one. Significantly, his description is not of Peggy, but of how she makes *him* feel. Foley seems to recognize Jim's self-preoccupation and he warns him not to go back to Peggy "or you'll look too closely." He also comments on Jim's possessiveness as pseudo-artistic, a point worth noting since Jim draws the women he admires and even thinks of Peggy as an "exquisite little figurine done with a delicate grace and belonging in some china cabinet" (137). Jim retreats to the pragmatic argument that he fits into Catherine's world after all, that Peggy is simply a "problem in understanding" (78). Foley points out that Jim may not have the right temperament to realize his ambitions (79). Thus the opposing social and psychological pressures build up in Jim's mind. Foley helps to water the seed of doubt in his heart that his social ambitions are not the way to find authenticity or validity in his life. However, he will continue to head for the top of the mountain against his inner compulsion to find a more spiritually satisfying path.

The Carvers show off their Renoir painting and talk about how painters can "put people and things in the right place in the pattern," while Jim muses on the inappropriateness of "the flaw in her nature that made her want to tamper with other people's lives" (82). In one of his few interventions, the narrator points out Jim's own error: "By rejecting and pitying Catherine's possessiveness he could believe he was free from the same trait himself" (82). When he cannot find Peggy, Jim looks for the little church in search of "a quiet solitary satisfaction" (84) but he cannot find her, so he broods (in one of the clumsier passages in the novel): "And maybe it meant he would miss Peggy too. If she had gone — with that door open to everybody — and if he couldn't find *her* either . . ." (85). He does find her at home and, after drawing her portrait, he hears the rest of her story about the Johnson family and her final break with her father when he confessed his loss of faith and she experienced her "whirling-away feeling." Jim's assessment is that she suffers from "false idealism" (94) and that the prognosis is bad.

Milton Rogers insists that Peggy is ignorant of the big economic picture and she is "grandstanding" in some way. "Besides," he adds in his best racist tones, "she goes for Negroes, and God knows how many! I'd be scared to sleep with her myself" (97). He adds that the Negroes do not want her around and calls on Elton Wagstaffe to confirm his opinion. Wagstaffe is more circumspect. He makes it clear that Peggy is not on any kind of crusade, nor is she simply trying to draw attention to her own goodness or the plight of the Negroes. She seems genuinely, unconditionally open to people, in his opinion. The problem is that she is indiscriminate; she offers the same affection and respect to everyone she meets. "So you see her standing on the street giving some no-good lavatory attendant the same glow she gave you, and you want to push him in the mouth because you know he don't rate it" (103). Since it is human nature for men not to trust each other, some men will convince themselves that she is offering sexual favours to some but not to them. That can only lead to trouble. Wagstaffe adds that she is a woman and ought to know better than to try to defy all the rules. Those women whose lives have turned sour get jealous that Peggy is offering men something they no longer can, and they want to destroy her. She creates suspicion and resentment; eventually she is bad for business (106).

Wagstaffe's explanation confirms Jim's impression that Peggy is sincere in her attitude towards Negroes and the poor; it also confirms his belief in her sexual integrity (108). The story makes him melancholy and bitter because, as he explains, she is blamed for treating everyone the same, while no blame is attached to the vicious, single-minded people who "have an itch to spoil her because she stands for something else" (107). In his view, people want to repudiate her because her goodness challenges their own self-image or even exposes their hypocrisy. His romanticism, once challenged by hard facts, pushes him to cynicism. The narrator intervenes again to point out that he is over-reacting, and then we enter Jim's mind as his romanticism soars to new heights:

> All these faces blurred into the sullen dark face of the trumpet player's wife. McAlpine forgot his own sensible unprejudiced attitude toward all coloured people and his rational good will; he forgot that they were working people out for an evening and no more malevolent than any white group in the other cheap cafés in other sections of the town.
>
> .   .   .   .
>
> He was called upon to be always at Peggy's side, persuading her, then taking her by the hand and leading her out of these places where she did not belong and into the places where she would glow with a singleness of love which would bring her happiness and not destruction; and in the places where he would lead her they would share more of the innocent lazy happiness he had caught a glimpse of the day he had walked with her through the snow to see the old church. (108, 109)

The words "called upon," "always," "take her by the hand," "leading," emphasize his sense of chivalric mission, his role as Orpheus in his own mind. His fantasy that Peggy will continually "glow with a singleness of love" and be happy is probably more pressure than she would welcome in her life! He seriously expects a life of "innocent, lazy happiness." When it comes to his relationship with Peggy Sanderson, Commander McAlpine seems to lose rationality, common sense, his contact with reality.

When Rogers informs him that Peggy's friend Wilson is being sought in Memphis for assault with a knife, he protects his Homburg against the wind and subsequently notices the charwoman's interest in him — possibly a reminder of the sordid or pathetic dimensions of sexuality. He washes off the "sordid life around that café" (111). A letter from his father seems to bring him back to his ambitious plans. He now analyzes Peggy's interest in the leopard and decides that he has "proof" that "her gentle innocence was attracted perversely to violence, like a temperament seeking its opposite" (112). He renews his commitment to what is "expedient" (113).

87

A climb with Catherine in her "Alpine mood" (116) up the mountain once again renews his hope that he will find his place in the *Sun*, particularly with her counsel. All the while he is with her, however, he struggles to convince himself that the "mysterious disorder" of Peggy's life, "the disturbing glow of a poetry in it he could never understand, alien as it was to his nature and shattering to his soul," will destroy his balance, self-control, sensible self-discipline and unleash "something in his nature like a hidden shameful wild recklessness" (118–19). Here is a character who does not know himself almost to the point of satire! Catherine now represents his place of "tranquillity and peace" as opposed to Peggy's "quick darting changes," (119) recalling the images of mountain and river in the opening paragraphs. When Jim drinks too much at the party on the mountain, he senses the shallow, garrison side of this community of the rich ("Why don't we all close the window for Mr. Havelock?"), and he cannot avoid the "disturbing illumination" and "the bewildering pang" he feels when he hears the words "stupid self-deception" (121). Still he is too embarrassed to admit to Angela Murdock that he knows Peggy. In the blue bathroom "cell," he struggles to understand why he feels ashamed, remorseful, insignificant, that "he had lost all his integrity." His answer is that he "had yielded up his respect for his own insight which had always been his greatest strength" (128). This is as low as he can possibly go. One senses that, for Callaghan, it is not his romanticism, nor his social blindness, nor even his ratiocinations, that condemn him. Rather it is his willingness to compromise his "belief in what he thinks he sees" (11, 17). What saves him is his inability to live with himself once he has done so. Now, at the climax of Jim's development as a character, "He cried it out in his heart because he understood at last that he loved her" (128). He seems to realize that love makes its own demands on him and that they are not necessarily consonant with logic, social propriety, or personal ambition. To yield to love unconditionally takes courage, faith, and self-sacrifice. He attempts in the next hour to break off his relationship with Catherine without hurting her (129). What he still does not know is *how* to love.

From this point on in the novel, there is a subtle shift of sympathy in Jim's direction. He witnesses Malone's threat of violence against Peggy. He reminds her of Wilson's temper. He soon sees the results of Jackson's assault on her, and he hears threats from Wolgast and

Mrs. Wilson. His warnings to her are certainly justified when he meets her again, and, one senses, his anxiety is motivated by loving concern for her well-being. Her indignant rebuke that she is not allowed to have her "own notion of your own integrity," to be "what I choose to be," is accurate as far as it goes, but it also sounds a bit hollow (133–34). She implies that Jim is simply interested in whether or not she sleeps with Negroes. This is somewhat unfair, as is her stubborn reluctance simply to clear the air by setting him straight, even if she does not love him. Perhaps she does not want to dignify his prying by giving him an answer. Her pride is understandable, but it would clear up any possibility of misinterpretation between them. Instead, she carries on an irrelevant defence of Negroes. She characterizes herself as a haven for "a lot of people on the run from what's inhuman" (135). This surely does not include Malone, Jackson, or Wilson. Why, if she knows they are violent, does she continue to encourage their attention? Callaghan begins to undermine her credibility while raising Jim's stock in the reader's eyes. This is not to say that Jim becomes a hero; he still clings to his projections, ambitions, and insecurities, but enough doubts about Peggy are raised to make his hesitation understandable. When he kneels to help remove the boots he has given her to protect her from the cold, the symbolical undertones of the gesture encourage our sympathy for him (135). Peggy acknowledges that she wants him around, that he makes her feel beautiful, all the while preparing to go out with Jackson. She will keep him around as a kind of pet, or bodyguard, or desperation alternative; he will patiently wait her out, assuming she has to fall in love with him sooner or later.

Once he has recognized his love for Peggy, he then places her in the best possible light. He worries that she is a beleaguered Saint Joan who will shatter the rich and the pious, and pay for it with her life (144). When Jackson, Gagnon, Malone, and Wolgast all insist that she is faking her racial sympathy in order to satisfy both her sexual preference for Negroes and her need for attention, Jim confirms his resolve to protect her from these racists (147). He offers his version of her behaviour: that she makes no distinctions based on race and is interested in justice and fairness for any of her friends who are treated badly. This is when they call him Orpheus McAlpine; he hears their derisive laughter as he leaves. He seeks her out immediately, tends to her bruised eye "with a gentle reverence" (151), and then tries again to make love with her in his extremely clumsy way. Callaghan spends some effort in this scene to depict Jim as a blind fool: "And his hand went out, thinking she needed only to feel the compulsion of his own desire in order to believe she had been persuaded against her will and so could do what she wanted to do" (151). His projection of his egotistic desire onto her personality is extreme here; and he thinks this way about a woman who has just been beaten up by another man! His declaration of love is undermined by his total insensitivity. This time she pushes him away violently and he finally understands that she does not want him. At this point, Callaghan shifts the reader's attention to Peggy's strange problem:

> His humiliation blinded him to the meaning of her anger. He did not realize that his kindness and love had broken through the passive indifference she had shown that day when he had tried to kiss her, and that now she had to resist and struggle not only against him, but against herself. He knew he had hurt her, but he did not see that he had done it by arousing her own desire. *He did not see that, if she yielded, she yielded also to him her view of her life and of herself.* He was also too bewildered to realize that she was now afraid of his gentle concern and his passion, and that it tormented her more now than any pressure all the others could bring to bear against her. (152, italics added)

Callaghan intrudes here to make it plain that Peggy's notions of all-embracing love are immature. She is now challenged to alter her notions of love from *agape* to *eros*. This is the most plausible interpretation of what, exactly, she is giving up of "her view of her life and of herself."[5] Jim characteristically reacts to his own humiliating rejection by turning it around and projecting it onto her: "And the cords in his throat tightened and his head began to sweat, but in his heart came one pathetic cry, Why couldn't she be a virgin? Virginity would be so becoming to her" (152–53). The word "pathetic" belongs to Callaghan exclusively in the passage. When he asks her directly whether or not she is a virgin, she coyly answers his question with questions of her own. Stubbornly, he plans to move into her room "to have her under the siege of his love" (155). He "would worm his way into her life and into her heart and take her life into his" (156). Later, he thinks of weaving a web around her (193). The military metaphor, and the association of the snake in the garden, or the poisonous spider, are part of indirect narration, so we can't be sure they occur to Jim; in any case, they make the point that he does not know how to love Peggy.

When he moves into her room to work, his situation becomes even more undignified. He tidies up after her, organizes her cosmetics, goes through her bureau, plants parts of his manuscript around for her to read, and helps her to prepare for her dates. He wonders "why she hadn't the sense to let him take her somewhere where they could lead an orderly life" (158), assuming that what he considers sensible, she should consider sensible as well. He insists that her untidiness is directed at him, not simply what she prefers. When he embraces her, "she would stand still, unprotesting, but uninterested, till her stiff stillness gradually took the heart out of him. Then she would smile to herself" (159). Jim does not see that smile, but the reader is forced to interpret what it means. It could be a smile of tenderness, but the context hardly allows for that possibility. More likely, it is a smile of triumphant self-congratulation at maintaining control over the situation and her independence, in which case the harsher judgements of her motives by Wagstaffe, Rogers, Foley, and the rest, gain a certain credence. In the meantime, Jim continues his dream of "remolding her," not realizing "that he was justifying her instinctive resistance" (161). How can he love her if he continues to expect that she will eventually turn into someone more acceptable to him? When he buys her Matisse prints, his motive is to bring her back to her own tradition (as he defines it), and to move her "in the true direction for her nature, toward what was light and gay and bold" (192). Here again, his definition of her nature, no matter how well intended, is an arrogant projection of what he wants for himself.

Wolgast's story of his white horse parallels Jim's story in important ways. The horse initially symbolized happiness and freedom to a child; it has now turned into a symbol of stability, comfort, pragmatism, security, and social acceptance, for the adult. Jim's ambitions are exposed for what they are by Wolgast's story, and there are small signs that Jim feels the pinch. The tableaux scene at the Montreal Forum provides Jim with another set of insights. The "maniacal white-faced mob" (182) objects loudly when the rules of the game are neither followed by the players nor enforced by the referee. In this instance, the Ranger forward fakes innocence and the hapless referee is blind to the offence until the crowd insists that the rules be enforced. Jim's reaction to the situation is to convince himself that Peggy is genuinely innocent, as opposed to the guilty forward, and that is a crucial difference. Callaghan's choice of analogy, here, is curious. He could just as easily have had an innocent, Ranger player defended by a fair referee against an unjustly insistent home-team crowd. The analogy to the Peggy-Jim situation would then clearly signify how we are supposed to respond to this unjustly maligned couple. Instead, he has the crowd insisting, quite appropriately, that the rules be enforced properly and the guilty player be sent off. This kind of analogy now leaves open the possibility that Peggy is, like the Ranger forward, a fake innocent and Jim is a blind referee. Moreover, when Jim previously imagined what the priest next to him would say to Peggy's confession of "uncontrolled tenderness and goodness" that paradoxically turns people against each other, he seems to mock the advice to look to "the greater harmony" (180). That is not necessarily bad advice. On the coldest night of the year, Jim asks, "How cold can it get around here?" Yet when he winds up hatless (aligned with Peggy who never wears a hat), he is angry and defensive. He denies Catherine's insinuation that he is quarrelling with the home crowd, and he wonders what he is going to do for a hat (183). He accepts Joseph Carver's Homburg (188) and finds himself at the foot of the steepest stairs yet (189). Callaghan evidently insists on looking at all the possibilities and complexities of the problem simultaneously; he does not add weights to one side over another to tip the moral balance. The hockey game tableaux does not definitively answer any of the questions raised in the story.

It can be argued that Jim's attempts to change Peggy's imagination by changing her room (193) are motivated by his protective, chivalric love. Peggy's refusal to be possessed by him, and her insistence that she be free to pursue her "sympathetic friendship[s]" (197) even in the face of possessive women, are her attempts to maintain her own notion of her own integrity (133) and her idea of what love means to her. Her acknowledgment, finally, that she has to avoid creating trouble between the Wilsons because that is "not good," indicates that she is beginning to appreciate Jim's concern for her (197). It does not prevent her, however, from going to the bar where she becomes the centre of the brawl that ensues. Jim's desperate struggle to rescue her in the bar, and his choosing to follow her home in social disgrace, are signs to Peggy that he is really on her side. He interprets her weeping as sobs of shame "over the failure of her judgement of herself and others and her bitter humiliating disappointment" (214); there are indications that, for once, he is right.

His Orphic words restore her self-possession (215). She now acknowledges that in her terror she heard Jim's voice: "A human voice. I knew what it meant. I knew what it said. I didn't want to hear anything else. *Just that one voice*" (216, italics added). Her knowledge of what his voice "meant" and "said" signals her conversion. She now knows that one voice of genuine love is as much as anyone needs, or can reasonably expect. The "sweetly normal" life she welcomes is no longer based on a general love of mankind. It is the normal love of two people for each other rooted in a vision not of possession, lust, or vanity, but of the expansive generosity and "caritas" which frees the spirit to "whirl away" from the pressures of social organization. She then turns the tables on Jim by worrying about his feet just as he had worried about hers earlier. She cleans up after him the way he had cleaned and organized her room. The difference is that she is not trying to change or possess him. She is willing, and (perhaps) able, for the first time in her life, to fulfil her love in sexual embrace.[6] "She watched him, wondering about him, feeling that she was nothing now, yet knowing she still had the security of his faithful devotion" (217). She feels that everything about her old self is gone. Her security is in her new knowledge of the nature of love between two people: ". . . the beating of their own hearts became their own world, and it was warm and good" (218). The icicles that represented danger all through the novel now begin to melt.

However, sadly, the beating of her heart "stirred up the old ache in him" and Jim begins to crumble. He is reminded that Negro men at the bar "had fought believing she belonged to them" (218). His deeply buried racism begins to surface. If he had thought of white men coming to her rescue, would he have been so troubled? His notion of possession also still gets in his way. When she asks him never to leave her, he tests her by asking if he can stay for the night and she agrees. Ironically, his insecurity about her is fed by her acquiescence. He tells himself that in her loneliness she might have accepted a "café Negro" if he had arrived earlier; the naked Johnson boy and Elton Wagstaffe swim into his consciousness. Callaghan is very clear about Jim's mistake in this scene. The narrator intrudes with expressions which indicate that Jim is denying his own best instincts: "they jeered at his insight, drowned out his own inner voice"; "feeding his doubt by deliberately misunderstanding her" (220). The other men's opinions clamour in his head, "twisted and tortured his thoughts, digging out of the depths of his mind the suspicions he had so resolutely suppressed" (220).

Jim keeps testing her and then interpreting her answers to work against her, until she reassures him that she knows how she feels (221). Still, he cannot hide his doubt about her behind his rationalization that she is probably just lonely and frightened and he does not want to cheapen her. The excuse even sounds false to him: "... and the sound of his own words was a bitter torment" (222). The narrator takes over at this the most important juncture in the story as he alternates from Peggy's mind to Jim's:

> "I understand," she said gently. There was a silence. With a compassionate understanding, she was letting him keep his belief in his good faith.
>
> But she had a new calmness. She raised her head with a shy dignity. The loneliness in her steady eyes and the strange calmness revealed that she knew he had betrayed himself and her, and that at last she was left alone.
>
> In the moment's silence he tried to grasp what was revealed in her eyes; he almost felt it, but it was lost to him in the anguish of deeper uncertainty about her acceptance of the honesty of his belief that he did not want to cheapen her. (222)

Peggy has just learned what it means to experience the deepest kind of love, only to sense a betrayal of it in Jim. Her love goes so far as to release him. Jim "almost felt it" (i.e. that she knows he is betraying their love with his suspicious doubts), but he is too anxious that she fall for his excuse to examine his deepest feelings. He puts his shoes on and leaves her. The faint smile on her face worries him a little and prompts his "inner voice" again to assert itself. He convinces himself to go back, but then he sees a "Negro boy [who] had appeared there like an apparition to justify all the jealous doubts already tormenting him" (223). He shoves the boy angrily and turns toward the glittering mountain, "and it had never been so dark or so high" (223). The narrator has clearly indicated that Jim has an "inner voice" that he is wilfully ignoring. It is not a matter of genuine confusion of signals at this point. Peggy has been an enigma to Jim and to the reader but, at this point, the narrator avoids ambiguity. Peggy's earlier behaviour, however naïve or imprudent it may have been, now works against her. Jim's wavering resolve to embrace what she stands for even against his class ambitions, takes over at the last second. His new knowledge of himself will appear too late.

Jim acknowledges his mistake to himself the next morning (228). When he then learns that Peggy has been raped and killed, he does not stay around her flat as a close friend surely would. At first, he blames "them" for getting to her; then her guardian angel for letting "what was good be the cause of her death . . ." (231); eventually he blames Wolgast's horse (244). The narrator dismisses his protests as a way of hiding "from his loneliness" (231). Jim even checks out of his hotel and hides at Foley's — an unconscious gesture of guilt. When he walks the streets, he feels, like Orpheus, that the women "were all staring at him with the same mournful reproach" (232). When Catherine identifies him as the artist who drew Peggy's portrait, Jim returns Carver's hat, insists that he is responsible for Peggy's death, and he weeps in what is a turning point for him. Both Detective Bouchard and Catherine are disappointed in him. Catherine slaps him for not living up to "that gesture of reckless, ruthless devotion" that would have been "worthy of him" (251). Bouchard offers him the excuse that the human condition is responsible for Peggy's death, but Jim does not respond to the suggestion.

He wanders around the cold city, "between the dark and the dawn" (254), searching for the reason he left Peggy. He associates it with the "the high dark hedge, the black barrier" (255). When he thinks about Bouchard's remark blaming the human condition for Peggy's death, he thinks again of Wolgast's white horse — now a symbol of social success and personal pride (255). He speculates that he "was always trying to change her" because he too had his white horse of ambition (256). He acknowledges that he has inherited the sins of Adam. As the sun touches the mountaintop, Jim imagines a crowd of men on white horses trampling Peggy into the snow as he jumps out of their way. Her voice in his mind asks him what he cares about what others say. Finally, he acknowledges why he left Peggy: "In a moment of jealous doubt his faith in her had weakened, he had lost his view of her, and so she had vanished" (257). The indirect free style used in this sentence fuses Jim's awareness with the narrator's commentary. It is likely that Callaghan meant this to be the final word on Jim's betrayal, and it is certainly consonant with his behaviour throughout his development. Peggy now becomes his ideal of love, and he sets out to find its incarnation in the little church where he first felt her special attraction. It is not entirely clear whether Jim recognizes that Peggy had come to a new realization about herself. That he does not find the church seems to be a form of punishment, but this does not mean that he will not or cannot ever find it. He seems to have recognized that he has to believe in different values — those that have been buried underneath his ambition and pride. In this respect, at least, he has been freed to love.

The minor characters function as social types. Joseph Carver is the corporate executive liberal hypocrite, insensitive to anything but power and prestige, who fires an employee for not following the tomato diet he suggests, and who blames the new generation of badly educated "Young Sloanes" for the ills of the economy and the country. The Murdocks and Havelocks, representing the established rich class, are presented as snobs and bores. The men of the Ear-benders Club are each given a background, but this is mainly to outline, in very broad terms, the variety of communities to be found in Montreal, and by extension to "universalize" the problems under scrutiny. The whites and the Negroes say they like Peggy, but most of them think that she is a fake and a nuisance. Their opinions function primarily to ignite the tinder of doubt in Jim's mind. Even Mrs. Agnew's remark about how much company Peggy entertains only serves to heighten suspicion around her.

Catherine is the only minor character who gains depth as we get to know her better. In fact, she may be the only character in the novel to merit the reader's sympathy and admiration. She has come through a divorce with poise and elegance intact. Foley's hint that she is cold or cruel (14) is discredited by her warmth with Jim, and although she tends to prescribe Jim's behaviour and friends, she is aware of her penchant for organizing other people's lives (82), and she obviously means to be helpful. Catherine fits in with her father's friends, but she does not blindly follow their lead. She sees them as shallow. She is sensitive to the shifts in Jim's feelings for her; she is subtle in her dealing with his moods. When she learns of his betrayal of Peggy, she blames him for not staying with her despite the fact that she would be the aggrieved person if he did. She is capable of "glowing ardently as she identified herself with [Peggy]" (250), and her disappointment in Jim after she recognizes his portrait of Peggy is a very poignant moment in the novel. She is truly one who is *lost* by the novel's close. She is a victim of Jim's ambition as much as Peggy is.

THE COMPLEXITIES OF INTERPRETATION

A convincing interpretation of the novel will depend upon how the elements discussed above are accounted for and linked together. Most of the critical commentaries accept Peggy as the moral centre of the novel from the beginning and then try to figure out what her version of love stands for — Christian charity, "life," intuitive altruism, etc. We have to keep in mind, however, the complexities of Callaghan's use of narrative point of view. Our version of Peggy as a representative of ideal love and personal integrity comes through Jim McAlpine whose ability to judge her is coloured by his own buried psychological conflicts and their related social prejudices. The view that Peggy is little better than a confused trouble maker, on the other hand, comes from men and women who are threatened by her behaviour, or who are jealous, or racists. Peggy becomes a vessel to contain the impressionistic views, romantic or hateful, of each of the surrounding characters. In this respect, she is the scapegoat she claims to be. Close scrutiny of Callaghan's use of free indirect style and irony in the way he manipulates narrative point of view indicates that he did not want the reader to sympathize too closely with either Jim *or* with Peggy until the last instant. The fact that we are often left with ambiguous interpretations of characters' motives and behaviours, and even ambiguity in the source of the commentary (does it belong to Jim in an interior monologue or does it belong to the narrator?), for the most part forces the reader to rely on his or her own wits to untangle the moral problems raised by the action. We have noticed, too, that we are not left *entirely* on our own, because the narrator comes out of hiding at crucial moments to nudge our responses in a particular direction. It is no wonder that the novel has been read as a parable *and* as realism. Callaghan has designed his style and story in such a way that it encourages both readings at once.[7]

97

Once we know that Callaghan's techniques force us to keep our emotional distance from all of the characters, we can then carefully assess those passages where the narrator intervenes in order to see what he means. At least a few issues become clear: the novel examines Jim's blindness and failure from a number of angles; it hints at Peggy's moral development in the process; it criticizes our culture for its bourgeois materialism and covert racism; it exposes the notion that some values that give our lives meaning cannot be approached intellectually. The novel is rich enough to support a number of themes depending on what questions are stimulated in the reader. We can examine a few of the most important themes; the list is not meant to be an exhaustive one.

1. The Nature of Love

The novel is preoccupied with what constitutes the highest love. It proceeds by examining what love is *not*, or what might be called immature or false love. Jim's attraction to Peggy, for example, is the result of his need for self-validation. Initially, his obsession has little or nothing to do with Peggy herself. He is not sure why Peggy attracts him, or even why he eventually decides that he loves her. At first he is simply obsessed. False love, the story implies, can start from an individual's need to believe in something outside of himself. This is all well and good, but it can take the form of a psychological projection onto another person of what a person unconsciously wants to believe in. Jim projects onto Peggy an unconscious wish for some romantic ideal of pure love untainted by self-interest, while he goes about courting Catherine for purely pragmatic reasons. His obsession for Peggy as an unconscious alternative to his guilt ridden ambition is a brand of narcissistic love. Thus, the novel implies that when love is obsessive, "fallen into," it is suspect.

Peggy's brand of love as "sympathetic friendship" is also given its shadow. Her romantic notion that one can love everyone equally is naïve and misguided. She nowhere defines her love as ideologically or religiously grounded; it is simply a vague, free-floating sentimentalism — a decadent secular version of Christian charity that started, in fine Freudian fashion, with a childhood glimpse of a naked Negro boy. Her subsequent appreciation of the family's closeness and joy as an antidote to her own arid upbringing is understandable. That

Jim should assess this as the basis for her interest in the oppressed is questionable. It certainly does not define her as a mystic or a saint. The criticism of Wagstaffe and Rogers that she is seeking attention is justified to some extent by her coyness: why does she take men back to her place at night, or tease Jim on numerous occasions? Callaghan continually criticized Marxist notions of brotherhood as romantic and naïve. He seems to undercut Peggy's version of pseudo-Marxist love as narcissistic in its own way, as well as being a social irritant.[8] She does seem to recognize the shortcomings of her notions of love when it becomes clear that she is the cause of domestic and community anger. She turns to Jim not simply out of fear or loneliness, as he blindly rationalizes, but out of a more mature acceptance of love for another for the sake of the other as well as for oneself. We have to interpret her conversion at the climax of the story in order to conclude that she has matured in her view of love, but there are clues enough to indicate a change in her, as we have seen, and we are directed by the narrator to accept Jim's retreat as a betrayal of something important.

The other kinds of false love exposed in the novel are less complicated. Possession of another is really a lust for power and control masquerading as loving concern. Jim's drawings, along with a few of his comments and his final confession (256–57), underscore this theme. Catherine seems to be possessive too, but she acknowledges it and presumably is willing to alter her behaviour if given a chance. Carver's concern for his employees, as Foley points out (78), is something like Jim's artistic urges — to grab something for himself. Malone, Jackson, and Rogers speak of Peggy only in terms of lust and putting her in her place. Jim's approach in his initial meetings with Peggy is that they are opportunities for his lust. Wolgast wants to protect what he has, and is willing to disfigure Peggy if necessary. Even Wagstaffe's attitude toward his singers is that they are possessions to be had for the right price. The worst manifestation of this lust for power and control is in racism. The white men are very sexually insecure when they despise Peggy for consorting with Negroes. They do not so much object to the idea that she may be promiscuous as to the annoying possibility that she would turn a white man down while encouraging Negro men who, they are convinced, would not be gentlemanly enough to stop if she coyly resisted them. Wagstaffe indicates that the Negro men have similar misgivings.

The most positive kind of love is only glimpsed as a beautiful "glow." The word is associated with generosity (5), openness and honesty of feeling (82, 191), love (109), poetry (119), and beauty (195). It is almost always ascribed to Peggy and Catherine. On one occasion, it is used to describe Jim's feeling when he is discussing his ideas with Peggy. It connotes an inner peace and relaxed self-possession. Once it is associated with the church (103). For all her imprudence and coyness, Peggy has a personality that attracts people. She is "fresh," alert, insightful in the way she quickly sees through hypocrisy and dishonesty. We know that some of her attributes are projections of Jim's need to believe in his own innocence, but many of the men acknowledge that she has a very attractive, friendly personality. Foley, Rogers, Wagstaffe, and others attest to her inner glow that seems to make people feel accepted for themselves. Catherine, "glowing ardently" (250), identifies herself with Peggy when she hears Jim's story about how he left her and we get the sense that women are in possession of this kind of love more naturally than men are.

Critics have tried to define the nature of this love. For some, like Hugo McPherson, Edmund Wilson, Milton Wilson, Patricia Morley, and Frank Watt, Callaghan generally writes about an undogmatic, nontheological, Christian idea of love because, as William Walsh puts it, he is an artist who possesses religion "as part of his personal nervous equipment" (Conron 1975, 152). Frank Watt, reviewing another novel, asserts that Callaghan's general intention as a writer is "to relocate the spiritual vision of orthodoxy — to find a secular analogy in the lives of his characters" (Conron 1975, 86). This is a fair summary of the approach taken by those who see in Peggy a saint whose love is from the beginning, ". . . a recognition of divine love which lifts us above the particularity of the temporal order into the timeless permanence of the One" (Conron 1975, 68).

If one emphasizes the images of the church at the end of the novel, which Jim knows he has to find in order to rediscover Peggy's spirit and thus save his life, along with the religious imagery of the novel (virgin white and blue, moon, water etc.), then Peggy can be interpreted as a thinly veiled icon of Christian love. However, one can interpret her final love for Jim as liberating her from a too narrow and sterile a definition of Christian love. Of course, ultimately, the two kinds of love, spiritual and erotic, universal and personal, need not be mutually exclusive. The novel seems to be presenting the possibility of their fusion in Peggy's last attempt to embrace Jim before she absolves him of leaving her to her sacrificial death. In other words, the notion of love with which Callaghan leaves us is not usefully summarized as "Christian love," unless we acknowledge that Callaghan has his own version of what this is. Peggy's sudden realization that she knew what Jim's "one voice" said and meant (216), has to be interpreted carefully, and ultimately, intuitively. As Judith Kendle points out in her article "Callaghan and the Church":

Thus, while his belief in the transcendent power of love and concern for the spiritual life of the individual are derived from the Christian tradition, Callaghan means something very different from *caritas* by love and is, for the most part, resolutely critical of orthodox, doctrinal, and institutional forms of Christianity. Not enough attention has been paid to the author's own disclaimer: "The last thing that's in my mind is to write religious books." (13)

Some critics go so far as to deny that there is any convincing rhetorical pattern promoting Christian love in the novel at all. One can make claims for its presence only in the context of the whole Callaghan canon.

2. *Individual Integrity versus Social Organization.*

There is a good deal of discussion in the novel about an individual's responsibility to fit into the "rules," "patterns," "order," of organized society. However, each individual has to "make up [his or her] [mind] about what we see going on," as Peggy puts it (17), and sometimes this subjective perspective pits the individual against the social order. If anything is certain in the design of the novel, it is that Callaghan favours the integrity of the individual over conformity to social conventions (the security and stability of the mountain) if a choice must be made.

There are passing references to a number of characters who are victims of repressive order: Walters has to follow Carver's diet or be fired; Wilson has been unjustly accused; Peggy's father has been so pressured by his parish community that he has lost his faith; Gagnon is under pressure from French Canadians to stop his caricatures of them; Detective Bouchard was "kicked around" for being too conscientious; Jim was in trouble with the university administration for his methods. Jim McAlpine is, in fact, introduced as a liberal intellectual who has written an article entitled "The Independent Man." He impresses the Carvers with his "quiet faith in himself," his "exciting strength of character" (5), his "absolute faith in his own judgement" and his "unshakeable belief in what he thinks he sees" (11). These obviously admirable qualities are put to the test when he meets Peggy, another individualist who also seems to believe in her own view of things. Jim, like his new mentor, Joseph Carver, is a hypocrite. Both men agree that "The world was in a philosophical breakdown, . . . a morass of mass thinking; the great trick was to recognize the necessity of independence" (28) and "individual initiative" (30). The "old-style, narrow-minded businessman" like Horton should be avoided (27), says Carver while he complains that an employee is insubordinate for not following the diet he suggested. Jim writes an article about "the lost men of Europe" who "surrender their own identity" (160) while he puts Peggy's room in order and dreams about how he will devise her life so that she will fit into his plans to join the society of Westmount.

The pressures for social conformity are symbolized by the incident at the hockey game in which the Forum is a "great black pit" on whose slopes "a maniacal white-faced mob shrieked at the one with the innocent air who had broken the rules, and the one who tolerated the offence" (182). The symbols of conformity to social conventions are hats and the colour brown. When Catherine chooses the brown dress over the blue one, it is a signal that she will side with law and order without question. As Judith Kendle points out in "Spiritual Tiredness and Dryness of the Imagination: Social Criticism in the Novels of Morley Callaghan," the prevailing value system of the society depicted in the novel is a middle-class business ethic which invades the commercial and intellectual elite and the small businessman and religious leaders alike (118). Carver, McAlpine, Jackson, Rogers, Malone, Wolgast, Wagstaffe, Reverend Sanderson, even the priest at the hockey game, are representatives of various communities and social classes. They are "the proud men on their white horses" (256) who oppose Peggy; many are suspects in her murder. The final lesson for Jim is that "what they say is unimportant, forever unimportant to me ..." (257). This is a post-war novel still very conscious that conformism to the enforced dictates of Fascists had led to the horrors of mass graves. Moral development can flourish only if the individual remains faithful to the "inner voice" which Callaghan implies that we all possess. We allow it to be drowned out by the shouts of the crowd at our spiritual peril, and perhaps, by extension, at our national peril if we settle for the mediocre, colonial status-quo and suppress individual vision and creativity.

Another important point that the novel makes, of course, is that Canadian society contains its own brand of racism. In the context of this theme, Peggy functions as a moral centre — a person who does not care at all about colour, race, or class. She resists even getting into debates about the subject. She makes the issue seem irrelevant. Both business and the church conspire to keep whites and blacks apart. It is not a case of one race openly persecuting another; the Canadian version of racism is to keep the races in securely locked social compartments of class and culture. Many of the Negroes seem to accept this situation because it avoids trouble. As Terrence Craig points out, the race issue is linked to the various communities represented in the novel, until "Ethnocentric pride employed individually to supply security and self-confidence seems to be Callaghan's rationale for racism" (104).

Callaghan was not an anarchist, though he admired the individual who never yielded to outside forces. He portrays the quest for individual integrity as extremely difficult to win, and dangerous to maintain. However he nowhere indicates that there is no need for order, or that the individual can challenge society capriciously. Civilized order is as natural as the patterns people make with their forks on the tablecloth or with their toes on the rug, as Jim and Peggy do respectively. The question is how does the individual *know* when to cling to a subjective insight and risk isolation? In an interview with Donald Cameron, Callaghan put the question this way: "How do you live your life so that you can roll with the punches, and still, in your own spirit, have this glow?" (19). What does Peggy have, at least at the end of her life, that the others do not have? The answer seems to involve faith in one's "inner voice" and intuition. The "whirling-away" feeling that Peggy experiences is essentially a commitment to one's own convictions about the right and good; a moral assertion of one's self in the face of enormous pressures from conventional mores.

This faith does not rest on intellectual activity. In the same interview, Callaghan registered his opinion of Jim:

> He made a mistake; I think he should have stayed with the girl. There should have been something in his heart that would override any attitude. When you're really good, you don't have to think. The trouble is, he *thought*. (25)

Order, systems, rules, harmony, are often associated with the male god Apollo, the sun or light of reason. Callaghan very often said that he felt women had an advantage over men because they were closer to giving life, nurturing and surviving. The goddess, on the other hand, is associated with nature, water, the moon, curved space and the mysterious labyrinth. Women are less idealistic, dogmatic, or prone to fantasy, in Callaghan's view. A woman will shift her position whenever necessary for her own survival or the survival of someone she loves. He felt this was part of woman's "nature" and her "role in life," as he put it in his interview at the International Festival of Authors in 1988. Doug Jones and others have placed Peggy with nature, the synthesis of opposites, the victims of order in Canadian literature. The women in Callaghan's novels, including Peggy and Catherine, seem to begin with an advantage. Therefore it is easier for them to maintain faith in their particular view of things. Jim forfeits his "inner light," as Callaghan calls it.

> I believe in this possibility in people. This business of disinterested goodness, the imaginative awareness of the wholeness of things, you see, is a most extraordinary thing.
>
> .   .   .   .
>
> And if you know nothing about human love, to me, in my stupidity, you can't know anything about divine love. . . . The Marxian materialist are like this as much as the Christians. (Cameron 22–24)

Peggy's initial perspective of love was more Christian-aesthetic and Marxist, in other words a theory of love, than when she chose to love Jim. Her shift of loyalty over to him baffled him and he retreated. He also failed to learn her lesson of fierce independence. He can only hope to succeed the next chance he gets, if ever he gets one.

3. *The Human Condition Question*

Detective Bouchard offers Jim an explanation for Peggy's murder: "What if we all did it? The human condition. That has truth, don't you think?" (253). Many readers point to this passage as the central theme of the novel. Bouchard apparently is to be seen as Callaghan's spokesman, and his question is, paradoxically, the answer. There are reasons to think that Callaghan designed the novel to lead up to this view. The symmetrical structuring of scenes and characters, the contradictions in opposing opinions, the image patterns which overlap, all suggest that Callaghan sees human nature as a paradox. Peggy wears both black and white. The white snow is both shroud and halo. The dark mountain is both beacon and barrier. Peggy is both a sinner and a saint, innocent and guilty, vulnerable and strong. Jim was attracted to her for dubious reasons, and abandons her for what he thinks is a good reason. What was a magical white horse for Wolgast, is the horse of destruction for Peggy. Her whirling feeling of liberation becomes Jim's whirling body (208, 212) and mind (220) at the height of his final confusion. The glimmering cross on the top of the mountain represents both redemption and death, love and loss.

The fact that Callaghan never does solve the mystery of who killed Peggy reinforces the notion that everyone had a hand in it; the one brutal man who committed the crime acted on behalf of a large group. If we are to accept this interpretation of the novel as the overriding one, then the novel is a rather pessimistic one. Perhaps for Callaghan, however, it is simply a look at the truth: human beings are capable of the most transcendent love and the most base brutality, and sometimes they can be seen to feed on each other. There are no firm distinctions and the challenge of living a full moral life is for individuals to step carefully and to hold on firmly to the "freshness" we were born with (Cameron 20). In this reading, the predominant mode is one of Irony that overwhelms the conventions of Romance.

There are obviously many angles of approach to *The Loved and the Lost*. The novel supports many answers, depending on the questions one asks of it. This is the mark of lasting art. The other mark is in its artistry. For all of its mannered prose, its unusual combination of forms, its lost central characters, it is a landmark in Canadian fiction because its artistry weaves beautiful kaleidoscopic patterns, while its transparent style and form conspire to turn our minds to the direction of our own lives. Callaghan seems to have wanted to write what has come to called "moral fiction" and has found the open parable his most accessible door. However, he knew enough of the modern spirit to resist imposing a precooked moral recipe on his reading public. That he refused to condescend to his readers means that he also made demands on them. In that alone, he reflects the growing sophistication of Canadian fiction after the war.

NOTES

1 These are by no means all of the conventions of these two modes; however, they are the relevant ones for a discussion of this novel.

2 The mode of tragedy has not been considered here because the essential features of tragedy — its inevitability, sudden reversal, new self-knowledge too late — do not seem to apply, at least not without ambiguity. There is no real purging of pity or fear, no irrevocable fall for Jim. Peggy is not the central character, nor is her fate tragic in any literary sense of the term.

3 Fables and legends generally depend upon personification and "moral tags" while parables contain metonymy, symbolism, and open-endedness for effect. Both rely to a great extent on dialogue. Callaghan uses the devices we find in parables and relies heavily on dialogue and monologues to make his points.

4 There is some controversy over whether or not the "style indirect libre" can sustain ironic statements, but most commentators agree that it generates an ironic stance on the part of the narrator. See Roy Pascal, *The Dual Voice: Free Indirect Speech and Its Function in the Nineteenth-Century European Novel* (Manchester: Manchester UP, 1977).

5 This passage was first recognized by David Dooley as an important insight into Peggy's character and into Callaghan's treatment of her. The passage is vague, as is everything about Peggy, and is meant, no doubt, simply to tease us into further possible interpretations of her motives and/or philosophical and symbolical significance. How far we are to take this passage as the final word on Peggy, is difficult to say since Callaghan never explicitly comes back to this idea.

6 There is evidence in the novel that Peggy may well be a virgin, though this is not a crucial issue for anyone except Jim. None of the men who claim they *could have* slept with her actually brag that they did. Among that crowd, they surely would have said so if it had happened. Peggy also fights Jim off physically as she must have fought off Jackson and will fight off Malone. It is consistent with her notion of "sympathetic friendships" that sexuality is irrelevant. She is immature sexually and tends to see sex in purely aesthetic and romantic terms. That she should accept sexual contact at this point is most likely the surest sign that she has matured in her notions of love.

7 Whether of not Callaghan consciously *calculated* this effect to grow out of his form and techniques of style is a matter of pure speculation since he did not critique his own style or speak of his intentions in these terms. My contention is that the novel achieves these effects all by itself. Hence the rather convoluted way of putting this sentence is meant to convey this notion.

8 There is an interesting aside in the novel when Joseph Carver registers suspicion of Angela Murdock's open door policy for her friends. "A little light from her lamp for everybody. All that's womanly and warm and gracious! H'm. Yet I find myself wondering. . . Oh, well — " (125). Carver is hardly a credible voice in the novel, but then Angela is not drawn sympathetically either. She seems to function as a parody of Peggy's behaviour, possibly to undermine Peggy's credibility too.

Works Cited

Annesley, Pat. "A Triumph over Isolation." *Telegram* [Toronto] 9 Apr. 1970: 58.

A profile of Callaghan including assessments of *The Loved and the Lost* by a number of admirers.

Bartlett, Donald R. "Callaghan's 'Troubled (and Troubling)' Heroines." *University of Windsor Review* 16.1 (Fall–Winter 1981): 60–72.

———. "Childhood Experiences in *The Loved and the Lost.*" *New Quarter: New Directions in Canadian Writing* (Spring–Summer 1987): 294–300.

Bissell, Claude T. "Letters in Canada: 1951. Fiction." Rev. of *The Loved and the Lost*, by Morley Callaghan. *University of Toronto Quarterly* 21 (1952): 260–63.

A very favourable review.

Booth, Wayne C. *A Rhetoric of Irony.* Chicago: U of Chicago P, 1974.

Callaghan, Morley. *An Autumn Penitent.* 1929. Laurentian Library 16. Toronto: Macmillan, 1973.

———. *A Broken Journey.* 1932. Laurentian Library 36. Toronto: Macmillan, 1976.

———. *Close to the Sun Again.* 1977. Scarborough, ON: Macmillan-NAL, 1978.

———. *A Fine and Private Place.* 1975. Laurentian Library 80. Toronto: Macmillan, 1983.

———. *It's Never Over.* 1930. Laurentian Library 13. Toronto: Macmillan, 1972.

———. *The Lost and Found Stories of Morley Callaghan.* Don Mills, ON: Totem, 1986.

———. *The Loved and the Lost.* 1951. Macmillan Paperback 37. Toronto: Macmillan, 1989.

———. *The Loved and the Lost.* Adapt. Charles Israel. CBC *Stage.* CBC Radio. 25 Dec. 1963 and 3 Jan. 1964.

———. *Luke Baldwin's Vow.* 1948. Illus. Michael Poulton. Richmond Hill, ON: Scolastic-TAB, 1975.

———. "The Man with the Coat." *Maclean's* 16 Apr. 1955: 11+.

———. *The Man with the Coat.* Toronto: Exile, 1987.

——. *The Many Colored Coat.* 1960. Macmillan Paperback. Toronto: Macmillan, 1988.

——. *More Joy in Heaven.* 1937. Toronto: McClelland, 1989.

——. Interview. "Morley Callaghan: 'I was loyal to my search for the sacramental in the daily lives of people.' " By Joyce Wayne. *Quill and Quire* 49.7 (1983): 14–17.

——. *Morley Callaghan's Stories.* 1959. Macmillan Paperbacks 13. Toronto: Macmillan, 1986.

——. *A Native Argosy.* Toronto: Macmillan, 1929.

——. *No Man's Meat.* 1931. Toronto: Macmillan, 1978.

——. *No Man's Meat & The Enchanted Pimp.* Toronto: Macmillan, 1978.

——. *Now That April's Here and Other Stories.* New York: Random, 1936.

——. *Our Lady of the Snows.* Toronto: Macmillan, 1985.

——. *A Passion in Rome.* 1961. Laurentian Library 62. Toronto: Macmillan, 1978.

——. *Season of the Witch.* Toronto: Exile, 1974.

——. *Strange Fugitive.* 1928. Laurentian Library 15. Toronto: Macmillan, 1973.

——. *Such Is My Beloved.* 1934. Toronto: McClelland, 1989.

——. *That Summer in Paris.* 1963. Macmillan Paperbacks. Toronto: Macmillan, 1986.

——. *They Shall Inherit the Earth.* 1935. Toronto: McClelland, 1989.

——. *A Time for Judas.* 1983. Scarborough, ON: Avon, 1984.

——. *The Varsity Story.* Illus. Eric Aldwinckle. Toronto: Macmillan, 1948.

——. Interview. "Who Is This Guy? Morley Callaghan." By Mary McAlpine. *Canadian Life* 2.1 (1951): 4–5.
Callaghan mentions the Orpheus allusions in *The Loved and the Lost.*

——. *A Wild Old Man on the Road.* Don Mills, ON: Stoddart, 1988.

——. *Winter.* Photographs by John de Visser. Toronto: McClelland, 1974.

Cameron, Barry. "Rhetorical Tradition and the Ambiguity of Callaghan's Narrative Rhetoric." *The Callaghan Symposium.* Ed. David Staines. Ottawa: U of Ottawa P, 1981. 67–76.

Cameron, Donald. "Morley Callaghan: There Are Gurus in the Woodwork." *Conversations With Canadian Novelists – 2.* Toronto: Macmillan, 1973. 17–33.

Conron, Brandon. *Morley Callaghan.* Twayne's World Authors 1. New York: Twayne, 1966.
Still the most thorough study of Callaghan's life and career although it stops at 1965.

——. Ed. and introd. *Morley Callaghan.* Critical Views on Canadian Writers 10. Toronto: McGraw-Hill, 1975.
A compilation of articles and reviews from 1928 to 1970.

Articles in this collection have not been listed separately in this bibliography.

———. "Morley Callaghan and His Audience." *Journal of Canadian Studies/ Revue d'études canadiennes* 15.1 (Spring 1980): 3–7.

Craig, Terrence. *Racial Attitudes in English-Canadian Fiction, 1905–1980.* Waterloo, ON: Wilfrid Laurier UP, 1987.

Deacon, William Arthur. "Stupid Montreal Girl Feeds Race Prejudice." *Globe and Mail* 25 Mar. 1951: 10.

Dooley, D. J. *Moral Vision in the Canadian Novel.* Toronto: Clarke, 1979.

Ellenwood, Ray. "Morley Callaghan, Jacques Ferron, and the Dialectic of Good and Evil." *The Callaghan Symposium.* Ed. David Staines. Ottawa: U of Ottawa P, 1981. 37–46.

Fulford, Robert. "New Audience for Callaghan." *Toronto Daily Star* 12 Nov. 1959: 28.

Details of the publishing history of *The Loved and the Lost.*

Gouri, C. R. "Society and Solitude in *The Loved and the Lost.*" *English Writing in the Twentieth Century.* Ed. S. Krishna Sarma. Guntar, India: The English Association, 1974. 97–103.

Disagrees with Woodcock's interpretation of the Orpheus myth.

Harrison, Dick. "The American Adam and the Canadian Christ." *Twentieth Century Literature* 16.3 (1970): 163–64.

Deals briefly with Peggy Sanderson whose death is "pathetic" rather than heroic.

Hass, Victor P. "New 'Racial' Novel Fails to Convince." *Chicago Tribune* 13 May 1951, Sec. Book: 6.

The reviewer dislikes all of the characters and thinks the novel fails.

Hoar, Victor. *Morley Callaghan.* Studies in Canadian Literature 4. Toronto: Copp, 1969.

Jones, D. G. *Butterfly on Rock: A Study of Themes and Images in Canadian Literature.* Toronto: U of Toronto P, 1970.

An analysis of Peggy as symbol of rejected world of nature and the irrational.

Keate, Stuart. "Montreal Nocturne." *New York Times Review* 20 May 1951: 18.

The reviewer disliked the story and characters as implausible.

Kendle, Judith. "Spiritual Tiredness and Dryness of the Imagination: Social Criticism in the novels of Morley Callaghan." *Journal of Canadian Fiction* 16 (1976): 115–30.

———. "Morley Callaghan, An Annotated Bibliography." *The Annotated Bibliography of Canada's Major Authors.* Ed. Robert Lecker and Jack David. Vol. 5. Downsview, ON: ECW, 1984: 13–177.

The best place to start any study of Callaghan up to 1983.

———. "Callaghan and the Church." *Canadian Literature* 80 (1979): 13–22.

Latham, David. "A Callaghan Log." *Journal of Canadian Studies/Revue d'etudes Canadiennes* 15.1 (Spring 1980): 18–29.

Malloch, A. E. Rev. of *The Loved and the Lost*, by Morley Callaghan. *Canadian Forum* June 1951: 70.

Matthews, John. "The Inner Logic of a People: Canadian Writing and Canadian Values." *Mosaic* 1.3 (1968): 40–50.

An analysis of how Canadian writers reflect the acceptance of paradox as displayed in Peggy Sanderson's character.

McDonald, Larry. "The Civilized Ego and Its Discontents: A New Approach to Callaghan." *The Callaghan Symposium*. Ed. David Staines. Ottawa: U of Ottawa P, 1981. 77–94.

McPherson, Hugo. "The Two Worlds of Morley Callaghan." *Morley Callaghan*. Ed. Brandon Conron. Toronto: McGraw-Hill, 1975. 60–73.

Morley, Patricia. *Morley Callaghan*. Canadian Writers 16. Toronto: McClelland, 1978.

A brief glance at most of the works for a simple thematic interpretation.

Moss, John. *Patterns of Isolation in English Canadian Fiction*. Toronto: McClelland, 1974.

———. *Sex and Violence in the Canadian Novel: The Ancestral Present*. Toronto: McClelland, 1977.

———. *A Reader's Guide to the Canadian Novel*. Toronto: McClelland, 1981.

New, William H. "In Defence of Private Worlds: An Approach to Irony in Canadian Fiction." *Journal of Commonwealth Literature* 10 (Dec. 1970): 140–41.

O'Connor, John. "Morley Callaghan." *Profiles in Canadian Literature*. Ed. Jeffrey M. Heath. Vol. 1. Toronto: Dundurn, 1980. 65–72.

Phelps, Arthur L. "Morley Callaghan." *Canadian Writers*. Toronto: McClelland, 1951. 10–18.

The first mention of *The Loved and the Lost*.

Ross, Mary. "Morley Callaghan Returns with a Memorable Novel." *New York Herald Tribune Books* 18 Mar. 1951: 6.

A review in which the novel and its heroine are memorable.

Sandwell, B. K. "The Hurt without Help." *Saturday Night* 27 Mar. 1951: 7.

This reviewer considers *The Loved and the Lost* to be the author's finest novel but the ordinary reality of the characters only skirts the edge of tragedy.

Staines, David, ed. and introd. *The Callaghan Symposium*. Reappraisals: Canadian Writers. Ottawa: U of Ottawa P, 1981.

Seven articles and a panel discussion offer new approaches to Callaghan's work and a wide spectrum of evaluations.

Stephens, Donald. "Lilacs out of the Mosaic Land: Aspects of the Sacrificial Theme in Canadian Fiction." *Dalhousie Review* 48 (1968–69): 500–09.

Sutherland, Fraser. *The Style of Innocence: A Study of Hemingway and Callaghan*. Toronto: Clarke, 1972.

Walsh, William. "Morley Callaghan." *Morley Callaghan*. Ed. Brandon Conron.

Toronto: McGraw-Hill, 1975. 129–54.

Watt, F. W. "Morley Callaghan as Thinker." *Dalhousie Review* 39 (1959): 305–13. Rpt. in *Masks of Fiction: Canadian Critics on Canadian Prose*. New Canadian Library Original, 2. Ed. and introd. A.J.M. Smith. Toronto: McClelland 1961: 116–27.

Weaver, Robert. "A Talk with Morley Callaghan." *Tamarack Review* 7 (1958): 3–29. Rpt. in *The First Five Years: A Selection from Tamarack Review*. Ed. Robert Weaver. Toronto: Oxford UP, 1962. 116–42.

Wilson, Edmund. "Morley Callaghan of Toronto." *Morley Callaghan*. Ed. Brandon Conron. Toronto: McGraw-Hill, 1975. 106–119.

Wilson, Milton. "Callaghan's Caviare." *Morley Callaghan*. Ed. Brandon Conron. Toronto: McGraw-Hill, 1975. 79–83.

Index